glee

GLEE CLUB
SIGN UP!

THE OFFICIAL ANNUAL 2011

The right of Charlotte Ward to be identified as the Author of the
Work has been asserted by her in accordance with the Copyright,
Designs and Patents Act 1988.

First published in 2010
by HEADLINE PUBLISHING GROUP

1

Cataloguing in Publication Data is available from the British Library

ISBN 978 0 7553 6165 6

Designed by seagulls.net

Printed and bound in Italy by Rotolito Lombarda S.p.A.

Headline's policy is to use papers that are natural,
renewable and recyclable products and made from
wood grown in sustainable forests. The logging and
manufacturing processes are expected to conform to
the environmental regulations of the country of origin.

HEADLINE PUBLISHING GROUP
An Hachette UK Company
338 Euston Road
London NW1 3BH

www.headline.co.uk
www.hachette.co.uk

glee

THE OFFICIAL ANNUAL 2011
CHARLOTTE WARD

headline

contents
special features

episodes

characters

glee
PILOT

It's a hard life being a geek at McKinley High. Languishing at the bottom of the food chain, daily life involves running the gauntlet of the school corridors trying to be invisible. Easier said than done. Tormenting the nerdy kids is a celebrated school pastime and the social outcasts are drenched in frozen drinks, dumped in the trash, heckled and harangued by their classmates on a daily basis. For a handful of them there is an escape though. Glee Club. A show choir where they get to perform with like-minded geeks and show off their true star quality.

When Glee Club teacher Sandy Ryerson leaves the school under a cloud, Spanish teacher Will Schuester, a former McKinley High Glee champion of 1993, asks the school's head, Principal Figgins, if he can take the reins. He forms New Directions and a handful of vocally talented undesirables quickly sign up: Mercedes Jones, who channels Aretha Franklin; Kurt Hummel, the fashionista falsetto; stuttering Asian punk rock Tina Cohen-Chang; wheelchair-bound Artie Abrams and determined diva-in-the-making Rachel Berry.

There are problems from the off. Rachel is unimpressed by her fellow Glee clubbers and demands that Mr Schue finds her a male lead to match her talent. Meanwhile Figgins threatens to cancel the club as he can earn more cash hiring the auditorium out. Will persuades him to reconsider and they agree that if New Directions qualifies for the 2010 Midwest Regional Show Choir Championship the club can continue.

When Will's efforts to recruit a good male lead from the football club result in ridicule from the jocks (and suspect names like 'Gaylord Weiner' and 'Butt Lunch' on his sign-up list) it's clear he needs to take drastic action. Sandy has confided to Will that being sacked from McKinley High led him to a breakdown and that he's now selling medical marijuana on the black market and forced a free sample on him, so when he overhears hunky quarterback Finn Hudson singing in the shower he vows to recruit him at any cost. The next day Finn is hauled into Will's office to explain why a packet

SONGS

'Don't Stop Believin''
originally sung by *Journey*

'Rehab' originally sung by
Amy Winehouse

'Can't Fight This Feeling'
originally sung by
REO Speedwagon

of medical marijuana has been found in his school locker. Fishy huh? Finn has a choice – he can either get kicked out of school or join Glee Club…

Rachel is delighted with her new male lead and immediately sets him in her sights as potential boyfriend material. But Finn already has a girlfriend – Quinn Fabray, president of the Celibacy Club and head cheerleader. New Directions also have a long way to go. A road trip to watch a performance by Vocal Adrenaline, the reigning national champions from their rival school Carmel High, reveals they have their work cut out.

Meanwhile Will's pushy wife Terri reveals she is pregnant. With a baby on the way she wants him to get a better-paid job. He duly agrees to hand in his notice and tells his shell-shocked show choir that they will have to carry on without him.

A disillusioned Finn decides to quit too but when a flash of inspiration hits him he returns and persuades his fellow Glee clubbers to work on a special song that will persuade Mr Schue to stay. As they practise, Will's colleague, guidance counsellor Emma Pillsbury, is playing him a recording of his own 1993 winning performance, in her own bid to persuade him to stay. So when he rounds a corner to hear the melodic opening bars of 'Don't Stop Believin'' echoing from the auditorium the breathtaking performance from his students strikes a chord. Mr Schue is here to stay and New Directions are on their way.

'I used to think that this was like the lamest thing on Earth. And maybe it is. But we're all here for the same reason. Because we want to be good at something.' Finn

glee
EPISODE 1
SHOWMANCE

The school's caustic cheerleading coach Sue Sylvester wants any extra school budget to go towards her champion squad and so she has a new prize in her sights – the total annihilation of Glee Club. It looks like New Directions could be totally doomed.

She summons Will to her office to tell him that his five-and-a-half Glee clubbers (including Artie 'the cripple in a wheelchair') won't qualify for Regionals as there is a minimum requirement of twelve members.

If Schue agrees to 'euthanise' New Directions Sue will make him her second assistant coach. Will refuses and rallies his Glee clubbers for a special performance in front of the school, which he thinks will totally attract new members.

It's a swell idea, apart from the fact Will has chosen 70s track 'Le Freak' for his kids because according to him 'everyone loves disco'. Err, helloooo? Even a bunch of misfits like the Glee Club know this is social suicide. But hey, Mr Schue is stuck in a time warp and won't be swayed. If disco won it for his 1993 Glee Club then it can reign supreme in 2010 too. What can we say?

There's no way Quinn, the alpha female of the cheer world, is going to stand by and watch a geek like Rachel Berry bag her man. When Quinn warns her to back off from Finn, Rachel fights back. 'Every day, Glee's status is going up,' she announces, 'and yours is going down. Deal with it.' Cue two passing jocks presenting McKinley High's very own Sandra D with a double ice-drink facial.

Rachel is bereft. Convinced she needs to be skinnier to snare Finn she is caught trying to blow chunks in the school toilets by guidance counsellor Miss Pillsbury. Emma has a few choice words to say about bulimia. Oh and unrequited love. Um, while gazing forlornly at married, cute, Spanish teacher Will. Sigh.

Rachel isn't giving up easily and promptly joins Quinn's celibacy club to catch Finn's eye. But the 'teasing not pleasing' mantra grates on her. She storms out after declaring that girls want sex as much as boys. Finn is impressed by Rachel's gutsy revelation although slightly distracted by his 'early arrival' dilemma. He secretly worries that thinking of 'dead kittens and stuff' isn't quite doing enough to halt the proceedings.

SONGS

'Le Freak'
originally sung by *Chic*

'Gold Digger' originally sung by
Kanye West featuring Jamie Foxx

'I Say A Little Prayer'
originally sung by *Dionne Warwick*

'Push It' originally sung by *Salt 'n' Pepa*

'Take A Bow' originally
sung by *Rihanna*

Back at home Will's pregnant wife Terri is demanding a bigger crib (of the house kind) which they can't afford on Schue's paltry school wage. So Will has taken an evening job as a school janitor. Embarrassing, much? Especially when Emma discovers him on his janitor round. But when she offers to help him, the lingering looks are a dead giveaway that Emma's crush might just be returned. Spying coach Ken Tanaka certainly thinks so. He wants Emma for himself but always has his advances rebuffed. Later he warns her not to pursue a married man when she can snap him up instead. Hmmm.

The day of New Directions' school performance arrives and the teachers and students assemble awaiting a freak show. But rather than stick with Will's disco track, Rachel has secretly convinced the Glee clubbers to give their red-blooded teenage audience what they want: sex. As the opening bars of 'Push It' blast out there are some eye-watering thrusting movements as a wanton Rachel straddles Finn and indulges in both teasing and pleasing. Will realises he has been stitched up like a kipper by his young charges.

Coach Sylvester is first to complain, suggesting the kids should all be put into foster care. Principal Figgins hands out a more fitting punishment. From now on Glee will perform a pre-approved list of songs that either have balloons or Jesus in the title.

On a high from the performance, Rachel lures Finn to the auditorium to warm up his vocal chords. After doing this the conventional way she leads him to a 'picnic area' and suggests he might like to kiss her. Within seconds Finn is in danger of 'erupting' and flees the auditorium.

Rachel is also heading for disappointment. If she thought she could land Finn so easily she's met her match. Quinn has joined Glee with her two cheerleader pals Santana and Brittany to keep an eye on Finn.

The defection of a trio of cheerleaders is at first met with fury from Coach Sylvester but then she hatches a plan. They will be spies on the inside helping her to plot New Directions' downfall. Mwahaha.

Terri's baby appears to have been snatched from the womb. A sonogram reveals her pregnancy is hysterical and she's not with child at all. But she can't bear to disappoint Will so instead decides to tells a bare-faced lie: the sonogram has revealed she is pregnant with a boy.

Back at school, Will continues to slave away in his janitor role and is surprised when Emma announces she is going on a date with Ken.

And at Glee Club a dismayed Rachel is crushed to learn that not only is Finn back by Quinn's side but the pretty cheerleader has nabbed the lead solo in Glee too.

My personality, though exciting and full of surprises, isn't exactly low-maintenance.

I'm like Tinker Bell, I need applause to live!

RACHEL BERRY

Age: 16

Super-talented Rachel won her first singing contest at eight months old and has been hell-bent on becoming a star ever since.

Her dream is a starring role on Broadway and she spends every waking moment making sure she gets there with a determination which is both to be envied and feared.

Rachel, who was raised by her two gay dads, isn't exactly one to hide her light under a bushel. In fact she never misses an opportunity to smugly showcase her talent – whether it be uploading a daily YouTube song or placing a gold star next to her name as a metaphor for her guaranteed future fame.

Sadly her gritty determination often results in ridicule from the other students (particularly the cheerleaders) and her shameless hogging of the limelight has made her unpopular with her fellow Glee clubbers – as have her incessant diva tantrums whenever she doesn't get her own way.

Rachel bulldozes her way through school life on a 'maximum intensity' setting for everything she does. She can be irritatingly self-centred and has deliberately embarked on fierce rivalries with both Kurt and Quinn.

But, despite her overwhelming personality, underneath she is kind and the first person to support her fellow Glee clubbers when they are facing a crisis. Deep down, like all gleeks, she just wants to have real friends who like, even love her.

Her single-minded resolution to be a leading lady is only matched by her desire to bag a leading man as well. When she falls in crush the results can be terrifying as both Finn

and Schue discover during her attempts to woo them.

After a brief dalliance with fellow 'hot Jew' Puck, Rachel thought she'd finally found love when she met Jessie St James, the gorgeous and spine-tinglingly self-assured star of Vocal Adrenaline who appeared to sacrifice everything to be with her when he transferred to New Directions. Hell, she even considered giving up her precious V plates for him. But she was left bereft when Jessie cruelly broke her heart and double-crossed her only to return to Carmel High.

Jessie wasn't the only Vocal Adrenaline member to mess with Rachel's heart. Their show-choir coach Shelby also orchestrated an elaborate ruse to help Rachel identify her as her long-lost biological mother.

Although at first Rachel was thrilled to have found her real 'mom' the pair struggled to bond, eventually agreeing to go their separate ways once more.

After an emotional rollercoaster Rachel has found her rock in Finn. Although he has messed her around in the past the gorgeous Gleester is clearly impressed by Rachel's astute ability to always know what he is thinking, combined with her go-getting attitude.

With him finally declaring his love for Rachel at Regionals it looks like bonny Miss Berry is finally going to be lucky in love.

Love interests: Finn Hudson, Noah Puckerman, Jessie St James, Mr Shuester

Rivals: Quinn Fabray, Kurt Hummel

Musical heroes: Barbra Streisand, Liza Minnelli

FACT! Rachel will only be shot from her left side.

WHO SAID WHAT TO WHOM?

To get you started, we've filled the first one in for you!

1 'It's just the way the light hit you just now, you looked stunning. No, you're radiant.'

2 'Why would you propose to me? You don't even like me.'

3 'We should join forces. It wouldn't take much. Just a little light making out.'

4 'Don't play dumb – you're too freaking dumb to play dumb.'

5 'Now I know what it feels like to date a baby.'

6 'What you call insanity I call inspiration.'

7 'You're a really good teacher, even if everybody is calling you a man-whore.'

8 'I fully understand if you want to beat me up.'

9 'You've got the pow, and I believe you should work it more if we're going to be an item.'

10 'Did I miss the election for queen? Because I didn't vote for you.'

11 'You're very sweet. You could be my second chance.'

12 'You could do a lot worse, and in this town you're not going to do much better.'

BONUS QUESTION
Who is the most talked about member of Glee Club?

Finn: 'I have to work so much harder to pretend to be listening to her.'

Santana: 'You can smell it on her – she's like a cat in heat.'

Brittany: 'Those sweaters make her look home-schooled.'

Jessie: 'I don't want her to get hurt.'

Artie: 'She's a total trout mouth.'

Answers: 1 Will to Sue; 2 Tina to Artie; 3 Puck to Mercedes; 4 Finn to Puck; 5 Brittany to Kurt; 6 Sue to Figgins; 7 Quinn to Will; 8 Rachel to Quinn; 9 Artie to Tina; 10 Kurt to Rachel; 11 Terri to Finn; 12 Ken to Emma; Bonus is Rachel

glee EPISODE 2
ACAFELLAS

Terri made Will agree to keep their baby news on the hush hush. Only Will blurted it out to his parents and now the lack-of-baby situation is getting to be a bit of a problem. Oops. During a chat with his dad, Will admits he's feeling scared about fatherhood. Daddy Schuester urges his son to have more confidence and says he wishes he'd believed in himself more.

Glee Club is tuning up nicely thanks to their additional members but their dancing sucks. So Rachel gives it to Schue straight: he's a great vocal teacher but his choreography is just not up to scratch. The Glee kids want to hire Dakota Stanley, a renowned Broadway choreographer. Sue is pleased with this news as Dakota's reputation precedes him and she is confident that the ball-buster will break New Directions once and for all. The Glee Club go in search of Dakota, finding him putting their rivals Vocal Adrenaline through their paces. He eyes the New Directions kids distastefully then barks that his fee is $8,000.

Will begins to reflect on his life. He wonders why he never tried to break into show business. He is distracted by wood and metalwork teacher, cough-syrup junkie Henri St Pierre, who has just returned to work after accidentally falling asleep and slicing off his own thumbs. As Henri reflects sadly on the fact he will never get to hitchhike across Europe, he and Will are joined by ex Glee Club coach Sandy, Ken Tanaka and Terri's Sheets N' Things co-worker Howard Bamboo – also musing about inadequacies of their own. As Henri begins to well-up, the four men softly croon 'For He's A Jolly Good Fellow' in perfect harmony. Will has an epiphany. They should totally form an acapella group! The Acafellas are born. Sandy immediately gets the chop though. The guys have voted and the group's too creepy when

SONGS

'This Is How We Do It'
originally sung by *Montell Jordan*

'Poison' originally sung by
Bell Biv Devoe

'I Wanna Sex You Up'
originally sung by
Color Me Badd

he's in it. At their first gig Acafellas storm it. Will can't believe his luck. Not only is his confidence rocketing but he's also irresistible to his wife. 'We started doing it once a week,' he reveals. 'It was like she was trying to make a twin!'

Days later and Acafellas are already in crisis. Howard's quit and Henri is in rehab fighting his cough-syrup addiction. Will decides to recruit Finn to join. His pal Puck also wants in – not only can he sing but he's hoping to catch the eye of a few of the older laydeez at Acafella gigs.

Meanwhile the Glee clubbers are trying to raise Dakota's fee with a fundraising car wash. As Kurt and Mercedes foam down his SUV she makes eyes at him. They've been hanging out for a while now and Kurt's been lavishing her with attention. She's convinced there's a spark.

But Kurt coolly declares he's in love with someone else. His eyes flicker over to his man crush Finn but Mercedes thinks he's looking at Rachel. She loses her temper and smashes Kurt's car windscreen with a rock. Ouch. It's not too long before the friends manage to bury the hatchet and have a heart-to-heart. Kurt confesses he's gay. He's never told anyone before but Mercedes urges him not to keep it a secret.

The Glee clubbers' first rehearsal with Dakota does not go smoothly with the tiny, ill-tempered choreographer scowling at the bunch of misfits before him. He immediately axes Artie for not trying hard enough to walk, instructs Rachel to get a nose job and dubs freakishly tall Finn 'Frankenteen'. The only three he likes are Quinn, Santana and Brittany. The others just don't have what it takes. Just as everyone starts to quit, Rachel finds her inner diva. Squaring up to Dakota she tells him New Directions are special because they're different. Then she fires him. Atta gal!

The Acafellas are warming up for a special performance at the Parent and Teacher Association meeting. Sandy has wormed his way back into the group after promising an audience with his 'penpal', best-selling artist Josh 'big brown eyes, cute as a buttermilk biscuit' Groban, who is looking for a new opening act for his tour. One performance of 'I Wanna Sex You Up' later and Josh is backstage. 'Stop e-mailing me!' he tells Sandy. 'Stop sending me nude photos... I don't know how you got my number. I don't want any more of your edible gift baskets or locks of your hair, and I don't want to read any more of those sonnets you wrote for me. That stuff got crazy, dude!' Josh slaps Sandy with a restraining order then heads off to chat up Will's mom, 'a blousy alcoholic'. Meanwhile Will's dad reveals his son has inspired him to finally pursue his dream – he's enrolling in law school.

Quinn, Santana and Brittany find themselves facing Sue's wrath. She's disgusted that New Directions weren't broken down by Dakota. 'I'm going to need you to smell your own armpits,' she simmers. 'That's the smell of failure.' Oh, but is it, Sue? We're not so sure...

FINN HUDSON

Age: 16

Finn has everything going for him; he's hot, he's the captain of the McKinley High football team and has a stunning (if a little chaste) cheerleader girlfriend.

With such a charmed high school life, Finn would never dream of ruining his reputation and joining Glee Club – but then a spot of blackmail by devious teacher Mr Shue seals his fate.

Before Glee, Finn had only ever sung in the shower – and that's exactly where Mr Shue discovered his talent as he crooned away in the locker room.

Finn loves singing but is terrified his rep will never survive a stint in Glee Club.

On the outside he rarely lets down his tough guy image, especially in front of the boys. He struggles to show his sentimental side, leaving him full of conflict and angst.

Finn has felt a void in his life ever since his dad died fighting in Iraq when he was very young. His mom Carole has raised him well but Finn pines for a father figure to guide him. He used to look up to his mom's ex-boyfriend, lawn sprayer Darren, but was left disappointed when Darren left Carole for a younger model he met at Pick 'n Save.

He went on to bond with Kurt's father Burt, his mom's latest boyfriend, but relations are now tense between them after the protective dad overheard Finn using slur words towards Kurt during an angry outburst.

Finn isn't homophobic, he just struggles to handle Kurt's more than obvious unrequited love – particularly as other students have noticed it too and tease him about it.

It doesn't help that Finn already feels sensitive around the guys. He was worried sick about his future after being outed as the father of Quinn's baby, then humiliated further when the real dad was exposed to be his best friend Puck.

Although he likes Rachel he worries that dating her will sully his reputation further. And feeling insecure, this all hits crisis point when Santana informs him he needs to lose his virginity and he allows himself to be persuaded.

But, as he experiences the highs and lows of Glee Club, Finn discovers that not following the crowd and standing up for what you believe in is more important than being popular, something Mr Shue firmly believes in. So when Will continually helps him to deal with the strains and strife of teenage life, Finn realises that his teacher is the father figure he's been looking for.

As he himself acknowledges: 'I didn't have a father, someone I could look up to, model myself after. Someone who could show me what it really meant to be a man.'

Fed up with picking on the little guy, Finn eventually leaves his days of dumpster tossing behind and shows himself to be a true friend to Kurt when he saves him from a beating being dished out by the school jocks. When Rachel starts dating Jessie he realises what he's lost and when they do eventually get together Finn is able to see that as long as being with Rachel makes him happy then who cares what anyone else says.

In his new role as a leader not a follower, Finn has at last realised that being a jock and a geek can be interchangeable and real men don't have to just play football, they can sing and dance.

Why does it always have to come down to me? Why do I always have to be the bigger man?

I didn't have a father. Someone I could look up to. Model myself after.

Love interests: Quinn, Rachel, Santana, Brittany

Rivals: Jessie St James, Puck

Musical heroes: REO Speedwagon, Journey, Kiss

FACT! When Finn is in danger of 'arriving' early he thinks of the mailman he ran over.

glee EPISODE 3
PREGGERS

OK, so seeing your sixteen-year-old son dressed in a unitard and gyrating to 'Single Ladies' isn't the easiest sight to behold when you get home early to watch the evening news. Kurt has been pretty much busted until Tina and Brittany volunteer an elaborate lie: Kurt is practising for his kicker role on the school football team. Kurt's dad Burt appears to have swallowed it but wants to see his son in action – at the next game. Yikes.

Egos are also being ruffled at Glee Club after Will presented Tina with a *West Side Story* solo to raise her confidence. Rachel thinks it should have gone to her and storms out in protest. She's largely ignored by her contemporaries who are getting pretty bored by her histrionics.

Meanwhile Kurt has managed to wangle a try-out for the football team. Finn cringes as he blasts out 'Single Ladies' and dances his way to the ball and the jocks snigger with disbelief. But then they spy Kurt's perfect shot through the uprights.

Meanwhile, Sue's big head is getting even bigger thanks to a new editorial segment on WOHN local news: Sue's Corner. But it's not long before it all kicks off when Sue discovers her new superstar status could be in jeopardy. The WOHN station manager has heard her cheerleaders are defecting to Glee Club. He warns her that if her cheerleading troupe doesn't win nationals her TV days are numbered.

So Finn, great news, your girlfriend's up the duff. Quite how this happened considering Finn's virgin status is questionable. Quinn conveniently has the answer: Finn 'arrived early' during a recent make-out session in the hot tub. The hot water helped his sperm 'swim'. Hmmm, that old chestnut.

Sue has a little surprise for Figgins. She's found an old video of him modelling anti-embolism stockings. Not the look a credible high school principal likes to rock. She says she'll kindly spare his embarrassment if he reinstates Sandy as a new arts administrator. When he agrees, Sue recruits Sandy to get Rachel to quit Glee Club. She knows the lure of a leading role in a school production of *Cabaret* will be too much for a self-centred star-in-the-making. Rachel takes the bait and Will is left fuming.

Back at Glee rehearsals Tina is struggling with her 'Somewhere' solo and she thinks Rachel should have it.

Will is distracted by a crying Finn, who is devastated about Quinn's pregnancy. With his chance of a future fading before his eyes he thinks his only hope is a football scholarship. But the McKinley High footie team are super lame. He wants Will to teach the jocks to dance so they loosen up and start winning. Reluctantly Will agrees and with Ken's consent Kurt teaches the team his dance routine.

Afterwards Finn confides in Puck, who immediately confronts Quinn. He says the baby is his. Highly likely seeing as he got her drunk and she actually had sex with him. As Quinn makes her way to her car her cool persona crumbles. Her tears are swiftly halted when she finds Terri sitting in the passenger seat. While Terri was trying to extract herself from of a web of 'no-actual-baby' lies, her sister Kendra had another solution. She says Terri needs to fake her pregnancy and get a new baby pronto. Quinn could be the answer to Terri's problems…

At the next McKinley High match the jocks are losing badly. There's only one thing for it: they need to spook the other team with their 'Single Ladies' dance. The sight of an entire team booty shaking leaves their rivals gawping. They capitalise on a gap on the field and Kurt secures the final point, as his proud father watches from the stands. That night the teenager finally confesses that he's gay. Burt takes it well. He's known since Kurt was three and all he wanted for his birthday was 'a pair of sensible heels'. Another result for Glee Club is that Kurt's help in the victory secures three new members from the football team: Puck, Matt and Mike.

Rachel smugly assumes she'll win back the female lead vocal but Will refuses, prompting her to quit again. It's all getting very Berry boring Miss Rach…

SONGS

'Taking Chances'
originally sung by *Celine Dion*

'Single Ladies (Put A Ring On It)' originally sung by *Beyoncé*

'Somewhere'
from the musical *West Side Story*

'Tonight' from the musical *West Side Story*

SUE'S JOURNAL

Dear Journal,

Feeling listless again today. It began at dawn when I tried to make a smoothie out of beef bones, breaking my juicer. And then at Cheerios practice – disaster. It was unmistakable. It was like spotting the first spark on the Hindenburg: a quiver. That quiver will lose us nationals. And without a championship, I'll lose my endorsements. And without those endorsements, I won't be able to buy my hovercraft.

Glee-e-e-e Club. Every time I try to destroy that clutch of scab-eating, mouth-breathers, it only comes back stronger like some sexually ambiguous horror movie villain. Here I am, about to turn thirty, and I've sacrificed everything only to be shanghaied by the bi-curious machinations of a cabal of doughy, misshapen teens.

Am I missing something, Journal? Is it me? Of course it's not me. It's Will Schuester. What is it about him, Journal? Is it the arrogant smirk? Is it the store-bought home perm?

You know, Journal, I noticed something yesterday. Of course, it's coming clear to me now. If I can't destroy the club, I will have to destroy the man!

Dear Journal,

Madonna. Simply saying the word aloud makes me feel powerful. Even in voice-over, how I have worshipped her ever since I was a little girl. Sorry, Angie Jolie, Catherine the Great ... Madonna is the most powerful woman to ever walk the face of the Earth.

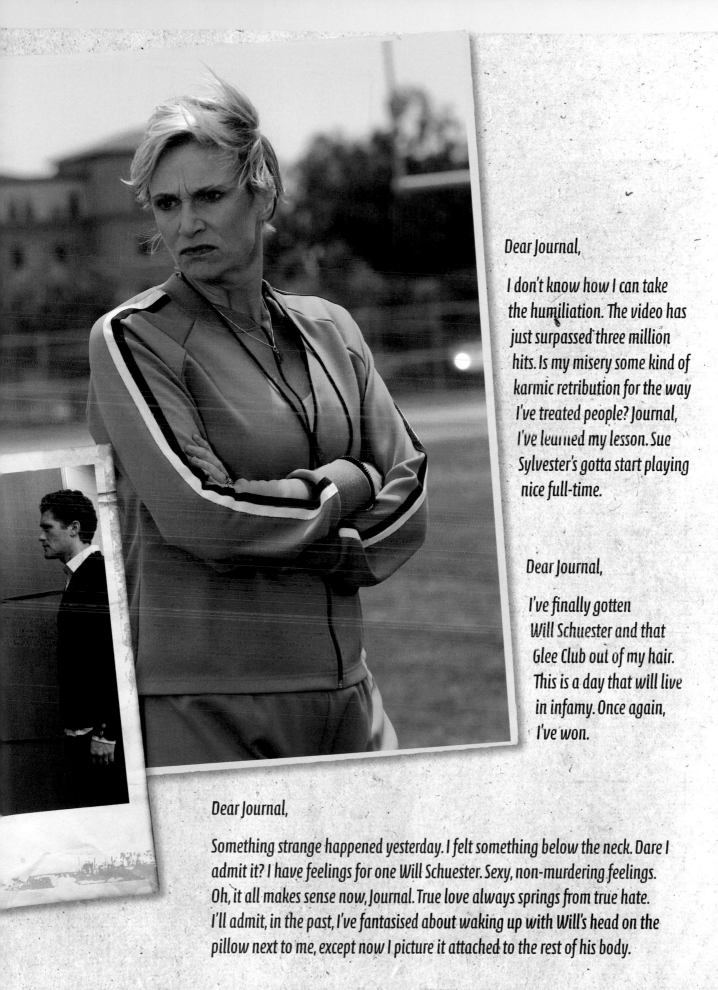

Dear Journal,

I don't know how I can take the humiliation. The video has just surpassed three million hits. Is my misery some kind of karmic retribution for the way I've treated people? Journal, I've learned my lesson. Sue Sylvester's gotta start playing nice full-time.

Dear Journal,

I've finally gotten Will Schuester and that Glee Club out of my hair. This is a day that will live in infamy. Once again, I've won.

Dear Journal,

Something strange happened yesterday. I felt something below the neck. Dare I admit it? I have feelings for one Will Schuester. Sexy, non-murdering feelings. Oh, it all makes sense now, Journal. True love always springs from true hate. I'll admit, in the past, I've fantasised about waking up with Will's head on the pillow next to me, except now I picture it attached to the rest of his body.

THE RHODES NOT TAKEN

SONGS

'Maybe This Time' from the musical *Cabaret*

'Alone' originally sung by *Heart*

'Last Name' originally sung by *Carrie Underwood*

'Somebody To Love' originally sung by *Queen*

With a Rachel-shaped chasm in their star quality the Glee Club are in dire straits until Will has a brainwave. He remembers April Rhodes, a former Glee Club starlet, who was a senior when he was a freshman but dropped out. After contacting April via her MySpace page, Will finds the ex-high school honey to be as gorgeous as ever – if a little alcohol dependent. As April didn't graduate she's technically still a pupil, so Will persuades her to return to school to finish her studies and more importantly join Glee Club.

April's arrival to Glee Club is met with a frosty reception, until she starts singing a breathy version of 'Maybe This Time', a song Rachel is also performing during her *Cabaret* rehearsals. April's performance moves Kurt to tears and Will advises her to try and bond with the students. She does this by plying Kurt with booze, schooling Mercedes and Tina in the art of shoplifting and showering with the jocks. An inebriated Kurt squints at Emma in the hallway. 'Oh, Bambi,' he murmurs to the doe-eyed redhead. 'I cried so hard when those hunters shot your mommy.' Then he pukes on her shoes. Icky. Cue a disgusted Emma berating Will for allowing 'bad influence' April near his students.

Finn tracks down Rachel and offers to help her learn her lines. She is flattered by the attention but Finn has an ulterior motive. Having given up on achieving a football scholarship, he wants Rachel back in New Directions so he has a chance of scooping one for music instead. Back at Glee Club Finn's been filling Rachel's diva shoes quite nicely and claiming 'Don't Stop Believin'' doesn't work without her.

At *Cabaret* rehearsals Rachel is clashing with Sandy and seeks sanctuary in the bathroom. She's caught crying by April and the pair square up to one another. April declares she has no plans to step out of the spotlight. The two divas then head separately to the local bowling alley. At one end April exasperates Will by revealing she's drugged up on horse tranquillisers and at the other a besotted Rachel takes full advantage of one-on-one time with Finn. April agrees to get back on the wagon and she and Schue sing an emotional duet of 'Alone'. Meanwhile Rachel is won over by Finn who says everyone misses her, coyly rebuffs her kisses and lures her back to Glee.

If Quinn hoped Puck would keep mum on her little dilemma she is sadly mistaken. As the other Gleesters gossip about Quinn's sudden bouts of nausea, Puck breaks the news but conveniently announces that Finn's the daddy. So, when Rachel announces her jubilant return she is largely ignored and hearing the news that her beloved is responsible for Quinn's bun in the oven leaves her shattered. Oh and she quits Glee again. Yawn. Storming back to the *Cabaret* rehearsals she urges Sue to oust Sandy and make her artistic director. Sue, of course, agrees.

It's the Invitational round of the Midwest Show Choir Championship and *quelle surprise*, McKinley's star performer April is drunk as a sailor.

She somehow manages to pull off a faultless rendition of 'Last Name' despite being completely pie-eyed but Will says he can't let April return to the stage for the second half. The show will have to be cut short. Cue a sheepish Rachel, who offers to be April's understudy. Turns out, being a lone star in *Cabaret* was a hollow experience and now she wants her friends back. She joins Finn on stage to pull off a smoking performance of 'Somebody To Love'. The crowd goes wild. Job done Gleesters!

'The house is packed – you guys are going to kick butt tonight. Your first performance in front of a real audience. I can't wait. You guys are going to love it.' Will

The only thing that gets me by is my knowledge that we are superior to all of them.

My body is like a rum chocolate soufflé. If I don't warm it up right, it doesn't rise.

KURT HUMMEL

Age: 16

As a fashion-conscious falsetto who can hit a mean High F, Kurt Hummel was never going to be a shrinking violet – and often battles with Rachel to bag the solos.

Not afraid to show off his unique style whether it be parading down the corridors dressed as Lady Gaga or wearing a corset to second grade, Kurt is extrovert, outrageous and proud.

Sharp-tongued and sarcastic, Kurt can certainly hold his own when it comes to the scathing put-downs, but he's not always as confident and self-assured as he makes out.

Kurt's mom died when he was six and since then he has been raised by his dad, Burt. For a long time Kurt was tearful about revealing his sexuality but after he rebuffs the advances of his Glee Club bestie Mercedes she helps him to find the courage to come out of the closet.

When he admits to being gay his dad isn't surprised, he's known since Kurt was only three.

Even with his dad's blessing Kurt still finds it hard to be himself and constantly thinks of himself as a 'disappointment', developing an inferiority complex when he sees Burt finding it so easy to bond with Finn over sport.

He even attempts to be the son he assumes Burt wants, dressing in flannel shirts and caps, and kissing Brittany, but his father urges him to do what makes him happy.

Eventually Kurt understands that his dad loves him no matter what. The same goes for his New Direction friends who respect him for who he is and what he believes in. Glee Club and his coveted role as official singer for the cheerleading squad have helped his true star quality shine. The school bullies may goad him, pour drinks over him and chuck him in dumpsters but that will never deter Kurt from being himself.

His relationship with Finn, the recipient of his boy crush, has also come full circle. After going through stormy times as Finn struggled to cope with Kurt's lingering looks (not to mention the shared bedroom after their parents moved in together) the two teenagers have formed a special bond.

Kurt knows deep down his feelings for Finn will never lead anywhere but, after a rocky start, he finds something he wasn't expecting – a surrogate brother who will look out for him when it matters the most.

Love interests: Finn (unrequited love), Brittany

Rivals: Rachel, Puck and the entire football team

Musical heroes: Lady Gaga, Madonna, Beyoncé

FACT! Kurt has an entire iPod shuffle full of songs from the musical *Wicked*

glee EPISODE 5
VITAMIN D

With Rachel back the Glee kids are feeling complacent about Sectionals especially as their competitors are a school for the deaf and a halfway house for troubled girls. Like, duh, how hard could it be?

A sneery Sue says Will needs to 'unleash the competitive animal' in his kids. Will duly challenges the kids to a boys-versus-girls mash-up asking each group to choose two songs and mix them together. The boys will perform on Tuesday and the girls on Wednesday. The winning team will get to choose the opening number at Sectionals. Unfortunately if Finn was a competitive animal right now he'd be an emotionally strained koala. The mortified father-to-be is permanently tired.

Meanwhile Quinn hasn't been turning up to Glee and her cheerleading career is in jeopardy. Coach Sylvester noticed a tiny buckle in her knee during a pyramid and is fuming. Sue blames Will and vows to bring Glee down – beginning with a visit to his wife Terri. It's about time Mrs Schue got the lowdown on her husband's infatuation with a 'mentally ill ginger pygmy with eyes like a bushbaby'. Sue suggests Terri gets a job as the school nurse to keep an eye on Will. The fact that Terri has no formal nursing qualifications is a slight disadvantage but she lands the job after telling Figgins she was in charge of the first aid box at Sheets N' Things and can use a defibrillator.

During her first visit to the staff room Terri is irritated to spot Will and Emma locked in conversation. With a cold smile she introduces herself to Emma as 'Will's pregnant wife'. Ouch. Her first patient is Finn who says he's struggling to sleep and keep up with all his school stuff. Terri prescribes pseudoephedrine decongestants to keep him awake. Next a distraught Ken comes to visit the nurse's office. He thinks Emma and Will are in love. Startled Terri immediately hatches a plan. Ken must propose to Emma. She hands him two decongestants, saying if he pops them nothing will stop him.

SONGS

'Halo'/
'Walking On Sunshine'
originally sung by *Beyoncé/ Katrina & the Waves*

'It's My Life'/
'Confessions Part II'
originally sung by
Bon Jovi/Usher

Finn is enjoying the frenzied effects of his 'Vitamin D' medication and hands them out to the rest of the Glee guys. The chemical boost leads to them performing a high-energy mash-up of 'It's My Life' and 'Confessions Part II' which leaves the girls open-mouthed. They speculate about how the boys pulled it off and then Kurt spills the beans. An angry Rachel accuses Finn of using performance enhancers to cheat, but when Terri also offers her a stash she is unable to resist. Rachel has persuaded Quinn to come back to Glee. Over the coming months she'll need friends – and they need good singers. So Quinn's there too when the girls pull off a hyperactive rendition of 'Halo' and 'Walking On Sunshine'. Now it's Finn's turn to confront Rachel. Shamefaced they agree it will be a hollow victory for whoever wins.

Terri's constant presence at school is causing Will stress. Being together 24/7 means they have nothing to talk about at home. Emma has a dilemma of her own when Ken proposes in the staffroom promising her a life 'clean of sadness and loneliness'. Afterwards she asks Will if she has any other options (hint, hint) then wades into an argument with Terri who gloats that she should stop pining after a man she can't have and accept Ken's offer. Emma says Will is kind and generous and deserves better than Terri. But Terri's warning clearly strikes a chord as Emma decides to accept Ken's proposal. She tells him that she doesn't want to change her name, live with him or see him after school. She'd also like to keep the marriage a secret. Ken, the love-struck fool, agrees.

Quinn also accepts a proposal – agreeing to give Terri her baby as long as she doesn't reveal the truth to Will. Terri is ecstatic but her joy is short-lived. She's been busted for supplying the kids with decongestants and Figgins is fuming. He tells Terri to resign and also throws the book at Will telling him that his obsession with winning has turned the kids to substance abuse. From now on Will will have a co-director for Glee – step forward one Sue Sylvester. Uh-oh.

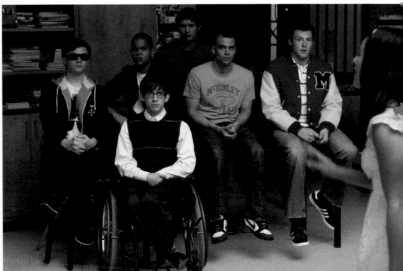

'Let me break this down for you, OK?
I empower my Cheerios to be champions.
Do they go on to college? I don't know, I don't
care. Should they learn Spanish? Sure, if they
wanna become dishwashers and gardeners.' Sue

glee EPISODE 6
THROWDOWN

It's Armageddon in the auditorium as a slow-mo Sue and Schue battle it out in a blazing argument. Their co-direction is not going smoothly.

Figgins has instructed them to direct a song each with the best being picked for Sectionals. The principal has warned them not to 'pit the kids against each other'. But hearing the ethnic minority Glee clubbers are unhappy with the lack of urban songs, Sue plans to do just that. Picking her team she hollers: 'Santana! Aretha! Wheels! Gay Kid! Asian! Other Asian! Shaft!'

At home that night Will tells Terri he wants more involvement with the baby. He recently drove Finn and Quinn to get an ultrasound where they found out they're having a girl. He wants to go to Terri's next scan.

Rachel has news for Finn. The school gossip blogger Jacob was going to break the news on Quinn's pregnancy but she bought his silence with a pair of her panties. Finn thinks Rachel is awesome but Quinn is not so sure. She also balks at his suggestion they should name their baby 'Drizzle'. And quite rightly too.

Meanwhile the war between Sue and Schue is getting nasty. Will has flunked several of Sue's cheerleaders in Spanish putting her squad in jeopardy. She retaliates by craftily snagging two more minorities: Jewish Puck and Dutch Brittany. Will is livid. When they launch into the mother of all rows their shell-shocked students walk out, tired of the showdowns.

At Terri's ultrasound her doctor shows Will pre-recorded footage of a baby and reveals that their baby is actually a girl. Will is overcome with emotion and cries, oblivious to the fact his wife and sister-in-law have blackmailed the obstetrician.

The next day Sue tells Will she is handing back the reins to Glee Club as it is 'too fruity'. But she leaves a departing gift – the outing of her star cheerleader. School blogger Jacob says there's nothing he can do. Sue found Rachel's panties in his locker and is forcing him to publish the pregnancy news or be damned. Be very afraid, Quinn Fabray.

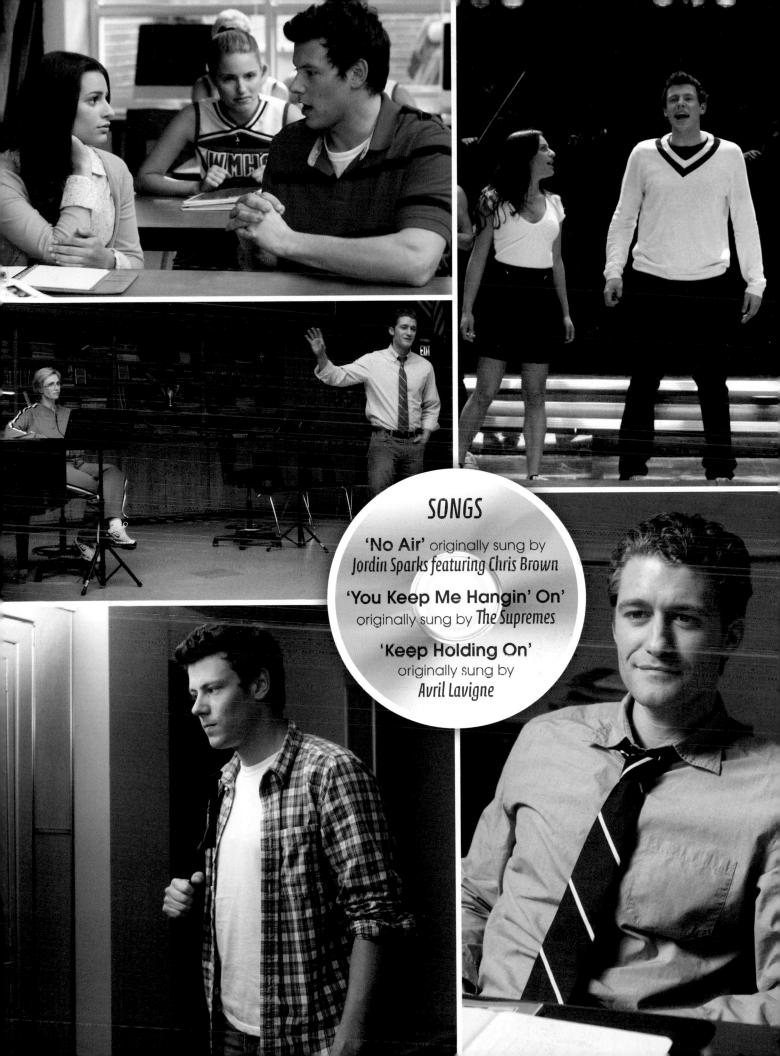

SONGS

'No Air' originally sung by
Jordin Sparks featuring Chris Brown

'You Keep Me Hangin' On'
originally sung by The Supremes

'Keep Holding On'
originally sung by
Avril Lavigne

MERCEDES JONES

Age: 16

Mercedes is a no-nonsense, honest and upfront diva who stands up for herself, her friends and what she believes in.

Confident that she has star quality Mercedes joins Glee Club keen to show off her 'Beyoncé' side. However she frequently gets frustrated by Rachel solo-hogging and the lack of 'urban' songs. She hates being a backing singer as her talent is as huge as her personality.

After her gaydar is seriously off kilter with Kurt, Mercedes agrees to date Puck for his 'great arms' but eventually dumps him for treating nerds badly. Now she hopes to meet a guy worthy of her time.

A terrible gossip, Mercedes can be totally indiscreet but she is also fiercely loyal and won't let anyone be badly treated. She's got girl power by the truckload so when Quinn, the girl she thought she could never be friends with, needs her help, she's more than up to the challenge and a firm friendship is formed.

When Coach Sylvester makes her a member of the cheerleading squad Mercedes loves the instant popularity that comes with it – that is until she's told to lose ten pounds and hates herself for trying to comply.

After fainting she tearfully tells Quinn: 'I'm so embarrassed. This isn't me. How did I become this person?'

Having realised that you don't need to be thin and uber popular to be happy Mercedes is soon back embracing her bootylicious curves and hanging out with the geeks she knows and loves best.

Love interests: Kurt (unrequited love), Puck

Rivals: Rachel

Musical heroes: Beyoncé, Aretha Franklin, Christina Aguilera

FACT! Mercedes designs the costumes for New Directions

Why does everyone assume I'm angry all the time? It's called being sassy.

I was a closeted diva.

QUIZ
WHO IS YOUR GLEE HUNK?

1

What sort of guy do you go for?
A Tall, sporty and handsome
B The brooding bad boy. Surely I can tame him!
C The smooth-talking, talented showman
D The unassuming geek with hidden depths
E The image-conscious new age man

2

What's his style?
A He's rarely seen without his football shirt
B A tight white tee which shows off his amazing pecs
C A sharp shirt and braces
D Indie boy glasses and a cardie
E Haute couture of course

3

What chat up line would you fall for?
A Do you want to watch the game?
B I'm hot, you're hot, we should totally hook up
C I want you to be my leading lady
D Do you want to come round and see my comic collection?
E Your cheekbones are divine. I'm totally making you my muse

4

Would your ideal first date be...?
A Hot dogs and a baseball match
B A foam party and wine coolers
C Dinner and a show
D A roller disco with good access
E A Lady Gaga concert

5

What is your first kiss like?
A He kisses you enthusiastically, looks pained and runs away
B You've barely puckered up before he's fumbling with your bra
C There's romantic music and lightning but it all seems a little staged
D He's cute and nervous but so are you
E As you go in for the smooch he kisses you on either cheek! Confused? Uh huh!

6

When you introduce him to your friends...
A He blushes really cutely when you introduce him
B He puts his arm around your shoulder but did he just check out your pal's boobs?
C He dishes out the compliments and your friends love him. But is he too good to be true?
D He's too shy to talk but smiles encouragingly as everyone else chatters
E He adores your friends – and raves about their designer garb

7

It's your one month anniversary – how does he mark it?
A One month? Has it really been one month?
B Welcome to Dumpsville. Population: You
C He presents you with a cute Care Bear but seems distracted
D He borrows his mom's specially adapted SUV and takes you to the drive-in to see a movie
E A voucher to get your eyebrows shaped. 'Yeti brows are like sooo last season.'

How does he declare his love?

A The love word slips out in the middle of a conversation and leaves him doing a goldfish impression

B I'm sorry I dumped you, I totally love you. Now will you put out?

C I love you but I have to keep you a secret

D He opens up about his feelings, and then tells you he loves you – for listening!

E I totally love you... in that dress

Mostly As: Finn

He'll be loyal to a fault but just don't expect him to share his feelings, especially if the guys are anywhere near. He'll pretend to be the tough guy but you know he's got a heart of gold underneath – if you can just dig it out. But if you're as emotionally stunted as he is, stay away! You'll spend all your time running in circles wondering what the other one is thinking and it's bound to end badly. You're going to have to be the strong one here because if you make the effort and force him to admit his feelings it will definitely be worth it!

Mostly Bs: Puck

Stop! Warning! Back away from the boy! You know it's not a good idea and as much as you tell yourself he'll change once he's with you, you know he won't. Yes, he looks like he's just walked off the pages of a magazine, with a six-pack to die for but he knows it, and you certainly won't be the first or last lady to see it. If you do go there it will be passionate, intense, and over very quickly. But once he gets what he wants, or gets sick of waiting, he might be off.

Mostly Ds: Artie

Well, you've signed up for a battle if you've fallen for this guy. He might seem like he just needs someone to love him but he's already fought adversity in his life and the last thing he needs or wants is someone feeling sorry for him. But if your feelings are genuine – and you can convince him they are – this one's a keeper. He'll be romantic and loyal but most of all he'll make you feel like the most important and attractive woman in the world.

Mostly Cs: Jessie

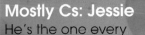

He's the one every man wants to be and the one every girl wants to date, but should you? Well, probably not. He'll seem like the perfect boyfriend but you'll never really know what's going on in that gorgeous head of his. There's no doubt he genuinely likes you, but he's also got a hidden agenda, and if you don't fit in with his plans you're probably going to get caught in the crossfire and end up with your heart broken. There's no doubt you'll feel very special on the way though...

Mostly Es: Kurt

Oh dear, you're not just barking up the wrong tree, you're in the wrong forest altogether. I know, he understands you more than any man you've ever met, he always looks fabulous and he gives you the best advice ever – but there's a very good reason for that, he's gay. Yes, sorry to break it to you but straight guys just don't come with amazing fashion sense, fully developed feelings, and the ability to express them. So, adjust your gaydar and look for a fantastic new man altogether.

glee EPISODE 7
MASH-UP

A thirty-two ounce 'Big Quench' grape-flavoured drink moves ominously down the school corridor leaving geeky students cowering in its midst. Finally the mysterious assailant arrives at their destination. Splat! Everyone gasps as school hunk and star quarterback Finn is drenched in the face with the sticky beverage. It's his punishment for 'insperminating the queen of the chastity ball'. A new world order has begun.

Elsewhere Emma and Ken's wedding plans are underway but they are struggling to choose a first dance. Emma liked 'I Could Have Danced All Night' but Ken has dismissed it as boring. He wants 'Thong Song'. They've asked Will to help them to merge the two in a mash-up dance and to help Emma with the steps.

At Glee Club the kids are unnerved by Finn's downfall but are distracted by Will who tells them they will be performing a mash-up for Sectionals. He wants them to come up with a song to combine with his favourite track 'Bust A Move'.

Later Will attempts to tutor Emma on how to dance in the long-trained wedding dress she has borrowed from her cousin. Predictably the train gets in the way and fells the pair of them with Emma landing on top of Will. They laugh, but what's this? An awkward lingering moment, secretly spied by a devastated Ken? Oops. Ken duly decides to punish Will by creating an extra mandatory football practice at 3.30pm on Thursday, exactly the same time as Glee rehearsals.

In other news Rachel and Puck are rehearsing 'What A Girl Wants' in her bedroom and start to make out. Puck's mom recently expressed a desire for him to date a Jewish girl so he's decided to pounce after having a dream about 'hot Jew' Rachel. The dream is clearly a sign from above that he should get into her pants. But Rachel isn't so sure. She still has a thing for Finn and feels she can't be with a guy who is yet to sing a solo.

But the next day Puck ups his ante sexily serenading her with 'Sweet Caroline' at Glee Club. Quinn and Finn both watch with jealous expressions.

Rather bizarrely Sue appears to be walking on air and is seen enjoying a jovial swing dance with Will along to 'Sing, Sing, Sing'. Her personality transplant is all down to WOHN anchorman Rod Remington who recently took her on a date playing Battleship and has invited her to a swing dance-athon. Feeling uncharacteristically nice she even tips Will off about practice ultimatum. When Will confronts the football coach, Ken reveals he is tired of being Emma's consolation prize and seeing Will lap up the adoration. He wants the kids to decide 'who is first choice and who is the consolation prize' when it comes to football versus Glee. Crafty.

It's not just the parents-to-be who will have to deal with making it through the school corridor without being submerged in a shower of syrupy frozen drink. There's a new target. Dating Rachel Berry ain't good

for the rep and as Puck walks arm-in-arm with her through school he experiences the wrath of the jocks. As Rachel helps him to scrub off the sticky drink he apologises for all the times he soaked her in frozen drink but reveals he will choose football over Glee.

Will accompanies Emma to the bridal store to pick out a train-free dress which they try out for dancing. As Emma sings along to 'I Could Have Danced All Night' gazing into Will's eyes he tears himself away. He dashes off to see which kids will turn up for Glee rehearsals. At half three the group sigh. None of the jocks have turned up. Turncoats.

But seconds later Mike and Matt arrive, swiftly followed by Puck. Only Finn is a no-show. Even worse we spy him moving along the corridor armed with a super-sized drink. He stops in front of Kurt but seems reluctant to throw it. But if he fails in his quest the other jocks will 'kick the crap out of him'. His indecision is ended by Kurt who grabs the drink and chucks it in his own face. 'Now get out of here and take some time to think whether or not any of your friends on the football team would have done that for you,' he chastises. 'Someone get me to a day spa!'

Sue is back on the warpath after discovering her new beau Rod making out with his female co-anchor after she'd invested in a snappy zoot suit for the dance-athon. Apparently they're not exclusive. Puck and Rachel also break up. It's obvious that she likes Finn and he likes Quinn.

Will gives Finn a pep talk: he needs to start making his own decisions like taking part in Glee if he wants to. It strikes a chord and Finn tells Ken he wants to do both. Finn returns to Glee with frozen drinks for everyone. It prompts smiles all round apart from Quinn. After being axed from the cheerleading for being a pregnant 'disgrace' she is sure that every day will begin with a sticky syrupy facial. But Will tells her the other kids will be there to hose her down. He clearly has no idea how horrible it feels to be soaked in frozen drink so the kids show him.

SONGS

'Bust A Move'
originally sung by *Young MC*

'Sweet Caroline'
originally sung by *Neil Diamond*

'I Could Have Danced All Night'
from the musical *My Fair Lady*

'What A Girl Wants'
originally sung by *Christina Aguilera*

'Sing, Sing, Sing' originally
sung by *Louis Prima*

TINA COHEN-CHANG

Love interests: Artie

Rivals: Rachel, Principal Figgins

Musical heroes: Lady Gaga, anything emo

FACT! Tina's audition song for New Directions was Katy Perry's 'I Kissed A Girl'.

Age: 16

Before joining Glee Club, Tina only had two facebook friends and kept everyone else at arm's length.

Painfully shy, the awkward teenager struggled to fit into school life, battling a crippling lack of self-confidence.

She dealt with it by creating a fake stutter so people would think she was weird and leave her alone.

But when she joined Glee Club Tina realised how much she was missing. Being in New Directions gave Tina the opportunity to feel special as well as a sense of identity and the courage to stand up for herself. She finally decided that she didn't want to push people away any more.

The person who's had the biggest impact on her life is fellow Glee clubber Artie and their strong friendship and affinity for each other appeared to be blossoming into true love.

But the revelation that Tina doesn't really have a stutter is met with anger from Artie who wishes he could just fake his disability and 'go back to normal' although he does eventually forgive her.

Indeed when Artie goes on to act in a misogynistic manner Tina shows her fiery, feminist side and puts him firmly in his place.

Despite speaking out more and more, Tina is still shy about her singing voice but with Mr Shue's help she starts to see that occasionally it's OK to shine and pull off a blinding solo.

It's also Will who sticks up for Tina when Principal Figgins tries to stop her from wearing her 'lacy demon clothes'. As the teacher astutely puts it, 'Tina is shy and one way she's found to express herself is through her clothes.'

Feeling stifled without her unique style Tina shows backbone and cunning when she stands up to Figgins all by herself and terrifies him into submission. Her goth wear is reinstated and it's clear Tina is finally beginning to believe in herself.

glee EPISODE 8
WHEELS

Finn and Quinn need cash and they need it fast. The bills for Quinn's scans and sonograms are mounting up and the fallen Chastity Queen tells Finn, who's totally not the father, that he needs to man up and provide for his baby. Nice.

They are not the only ones strapped for dosh. Glee Club need to rent a special bus to take wheelchair-bound Artie to Sectionals but Figgins won't cough up. Will says New Directions will have to raise the money themselves. Sadly the kids don't share his enthusiasm, suggesting rather meanly that Artie's dad could drive him as usual. Artie is clearly hurt by their lack of camaraderie but shrugs it off.

It's song time and the sheet music is handed out for musical theatre number 'Defying Gravity' to Wicked fan Kurt's delight. Yet Will decides that Rachel should have the solo. He reasons that the song is meant for a female singer. Kurt's dad doesn't agree and pays Figgins a visit by saying his son is being discriminated against and should be allowed to audition to sing the song. Will agrees that Rachel and Kurt can go head to head to audition with the other kids voting to decide who scoops the song.

With the kids reacting uncharitably to his suggestions of raising money for Artie's bus with a bake sale, Will presents each of them with their own wheelchair. He informs the perplexed pupils that they will now spend three hours experiencing life in Artie's shoes and putting together a 'wheelchair number'.

Meanwhile Puck surprises Quinn with eighteen dollars. He knows she is struggling and wants to help. Although she is scornful at first, she softens and they are about to kiss when Finn rocks up. Later Puck picks a fight with Finn, laying into him for not providing for his baby. They start to kick and punch in their wheelchairs until Will wades in. Finn can't understand why Puck is so angry.

SONGS

'Defying Gravity'
from the musical *Wicked*

'Dancing With Myself'
originally sung by *Billy Idol*

'Proud Mary' originally
sung by *Creedence
Clearwater Revival*

Figgins is inspired by the new equal opportunities drive at Glee and tells a belligerent Sue she must hold school-wide auditions to fill Quinn's place in the squad. He sends Will to judge that no one is discriminated against. When Brittany's friend Becky, a pupil with Down's Syndrome who Brittany cheats off in math class, comes in to audition, Will urges Sue to be nice. Becky jumps rope badly but Sue tells her practice begins at 4pm. She's in the squad and Will smells a rat.

Meanwhile Artie is doing a sterling job teaching the kids his best wheelchair dance moves ready for their assignment song 'Proud Mary'. Things have been getting pretty flirty with him and Tina for a while and afterwards they have a heart-to-heart. Tina says she admires him and Artie reveals how he was crippled in a car crash aged eight. He reassures her that while his legs don't work his penis does. Blush!

A new batch of cakes baked by Puck are going down a storm at the bake sale. The secret ingredient? A pinch of medical marijuana to give you 'a wicked case of the munchies'.

At Glee Club the all-important sing-off begins with Kurt giving Rachel stiff competition right until the end when he blows the High F, which he's been practising. Rachel's performance is flawless and she wins the song.

Meanwhile Puck tells Quinn he wants to be a good father and provider and offers her the cash for her medical bills. Quinn is impressed but says the money has to go towards the bus for Artie. Finn also has a wad of cash for Quinn. He's had his first pay cheque from a local restaurant. He got a job working in the restaurant in his wheelchair after Rachel told the manager that not hiring Finn could be seen as discrimination.

When Puck hands over the bake sale proceeds to Glee Club, Artie says he'd prefer to spend the money on a wheelchair ramp to improve access to the auditorium. But cash has already been allocated for three new ramps. Sue has written Figgins a cheque to cover it. Her benevolent attitude is leaving Will flummoxed. All becomes clear when Sue visits the nursing home where her sister Jean is a resident. It turns out Jean has Down's Syndrome and the siblings are very close.

After racing playfully up and down the school corridors in their wheelchairs Artie and Tina have their first kiss. But then Tina drops a bombshell. She's been faking her stutter since sixth grade. She says she did it because she's shy and it made people leave her alone. But Artie reacts angrily. He thought they had something really important in common and wheels off alone.

Burt was angry at receiving a mystery phone call from a man calling Kurt a fag. Although Burt supported Kurt's decision to sing the *Wicked* song he was concerned for his son's safety. It turns out, Kurt deliberately messed up the high note in his audition so Rachel would get the song. While he is proud to be gay he doesn't want his father to experience the ridicule that singing a girl's song would inevitably bring to them. 'I love you more than I love being a star,' he tells his dad. Aww.

glee EPISODE 9
BALLAD

It's all change at Sectionals and the rule book now states that show choirs must include a ballad in their two-song set. Brittany is confused. She thinks that a ballad is a male duck but Will sets her straight. A ballad is a story set to music that conveys your feelings.

He pairs everyone into groups to work on songs but with Mike off sick (having a spider extracted from his ear – ugh) Rachel is left out. Will agrees to sing with her with a slight sense of foreboding. The hormonally charged teenager immediately chooses 'Endless Love', a song that Will considers inappropriate for a student and teacher but finds himself bamboozled into singing. As they start to duet together Will's reservations about the song are clearly founded. Rachel starts to gaze at him and Will is worried. It's not the first time he's had to deal with a schoolgirl crush.

Uh-oh, looks like Rachel is a gonner: 'It's like I'm seeing him for the first time and what I'm seeing is super, super cute.' Cue the besotted schoolgirl arriving in Will's classroom with a love token – a tie with stars and a treble clef motif. For Schue it brings back memories of another smitten student, Suzy Pepper. When he rebuffed Suzy's advances her cry for help was to munch on the world's hottest pepper. She ended up in a medically induced coma for three days.

Meanwhile Finn and Kurt are working on their ballad. Kurt loves having the object of his undying affection to himself but Finn is struggling to sing to 'a dude'. Kurt encourages him to imagine he's singing to his unborn daughter. That night his mom catches him singing 'I'll Stand By You' to a sonogram on his laptop. When she asks him if Quinn is pregnant he dissolves into tears. Finn's mom tells him that it will all be OK.

Operation Let Rachel Down Gently is underway. Emma thinks Will should serenade Rachel with a song that puts her straight – and agrees to sit in while he sings it. Will's cautionary tale begins through the mash-up medium of 'Young Girl' and 'Don't Stand So Close To Me'. But has Rachel got the message? 'I'm very young and it's hard for you to stand so close to me,' she gabbles jubilantly. Judging by the lovestruck look on Emma's face it hasn't discouraged her either.

Later when Will arrives home he is horrified to find Rachel there – and that Terri has put her to work cooking and cleaning. 'Look, I have been dealing with these schoolgirl crushes for years,' snaps Terri. 'Why shouldn't I get a little something out of it?' Packing Rachel into the car Will immediately drives her home cringing as she attempts to serenade him with 'Crush'. There is no reasoning with her. The next day at school she is met by Suzy Pepper who warns her to stay away or she'll get hurt real bad.

Later as Mercedes and Puck work on a song together she reveals that the group are planning to sing a ballad to Finn and Quinn to show their support. A peeved Puck blurts out that the baby is actually his. Mercedes warns him that Quinn chose Finn and that he needs to accept it.

Meanwhile a nervous Finn is dining with the Fabrays on Quinn's father's request. Kurt has helped him pick out an outfit but the evening is getting increasingly fraught for Finn. Dashing to the loo he calls Kurt who advises him to go ahead with the special ballad they've rehearsed.

He heads back and tells Quinn's parents he'd like to sing something to express his feelings. With the CD lined up he begins to serenade a horrified Quinn with '(You're) Having My Baby'. The Fabrays finally twig that their daughter is not so virtuous after all and Quinn's father kicks her out with her mother failing to intervene. Finn takes a tearful Quinn home to his mom.

Scary Suzy approaches Rachel again revealing that they aren't so different. After two years of intense psychotherapy and an oesophagus transplant she has learnt that crushing on guys who will never like you back only leads to low self-esteem. When Rachel sees Will she immediately apologises for being inappropriate. She wants to sing 'Sorry Seems To Be The Hardest Word'. Will says she'll meet a boy her own age who will like her for everything she is.

Finn fills Kurt in on the Fabray debacle and admits he is happy that the pregnancy is out in the open. Kurt had secretly hoped it would all go wrong, leaving Finn to cry on his shoulder but decides he's happy because Finn is happy.

The Glee Club then serenade Quinn and Finn with their surprise ballad to show their support – a rendition of 'Lean On Me'. Bless.

SONGS

'I'll Stand By You'
originally sung by *The Pretenders*

'Endless Love' originally sung by
Diana Ross and Lionel Richie

'Crush' originally sung by *Jennifer Paige*

'Don't Stand So Close To Me'/'Young Girl'
originally sung by *The Police/Gary Puckett & The Union Gap*

'(You're) Having My Baby'
originally sung by *Paul Anka and Odia Coates*

'Lean On Me'
originally sung by *Bill Withers*

QUINN FABRAY

Age: 16

Quinn Fabray once lived a charmed life. She was the most popular girl in school, president of the celibacy club, chief cheerleader and all the guys fancied her.

On paper there really could not have been a worse fate than getting pregnant by the school casanova and being ditched from the cheerleading team.

But in many ways getting knocked up by Puck, the best friend of her boyfriend Finn, was also the best thing to happen to Quinn.

In no particular order she is kinder, happier and healthier than her previous un-impregnated self.

Before her downfall the pretty but cold star cheerleader spent her time being bitchy, obsessing over her weight and cultivating her reputation. Flanked by a gaggle of bitchy cheerleaders she was the Queen of Mean, writing slurs on toilet walls and the chief thrower of drinks at the nerds.

She may have originally joined Glee to spy for Sue, and keep an eye on her boyfriend Finn, but soon Quinn begins to find the values and camaraderie of show choir infectious.

Although she treats Finn abysmally – letting him think he is her baby's father even though they've never had sex – getting pregnant at sixteen also makes Quinn grow up quickly. She starts to get perspective. As her world crumbles around her, her parents disown her in shame and Sue Sylvester berates her, it is New Directions – the kids she previously bullied and taunted – that prove to be her loyal friends.

She sees that winning isn't the be-all and end-all and starts to care about the other members. When she sees Mercedes desperately slimming she urges her to stop, telling her she's beautiful.

As she says: 'When you start eating for somebody else, so that they can grow and be healthy, your relationship to food changes. What I realised is that if I'm so willing to eat right to take care of this baby, why am I not willing to do it for myself?'

Whereas previously Quinn had a one-dimensional view of the world where people were either cool or not, she now knows how first impressions can be wrong.

She is surprised by the way Puck has manned up to his fatherhood responsibility and is touched by Mercedes' kindness in offering her a place to stay.

Making the decision to give up baby Beth wasn't easy but Quinn is adamant it was the right one and is now ready to return to her old life as a wiser, nicer person. Well, we live in hope...

Love interests: Finn, Puck

Rivals: Rachel, Santana

Musical heroes: Madonna, Dionne Warwick

FACT! Quinn's celibacy club was called Christ Crusaders

A bad reputation is better than no reputation at all.

Status is like currency. When your bank account is full, you can get away with doing just about anything.

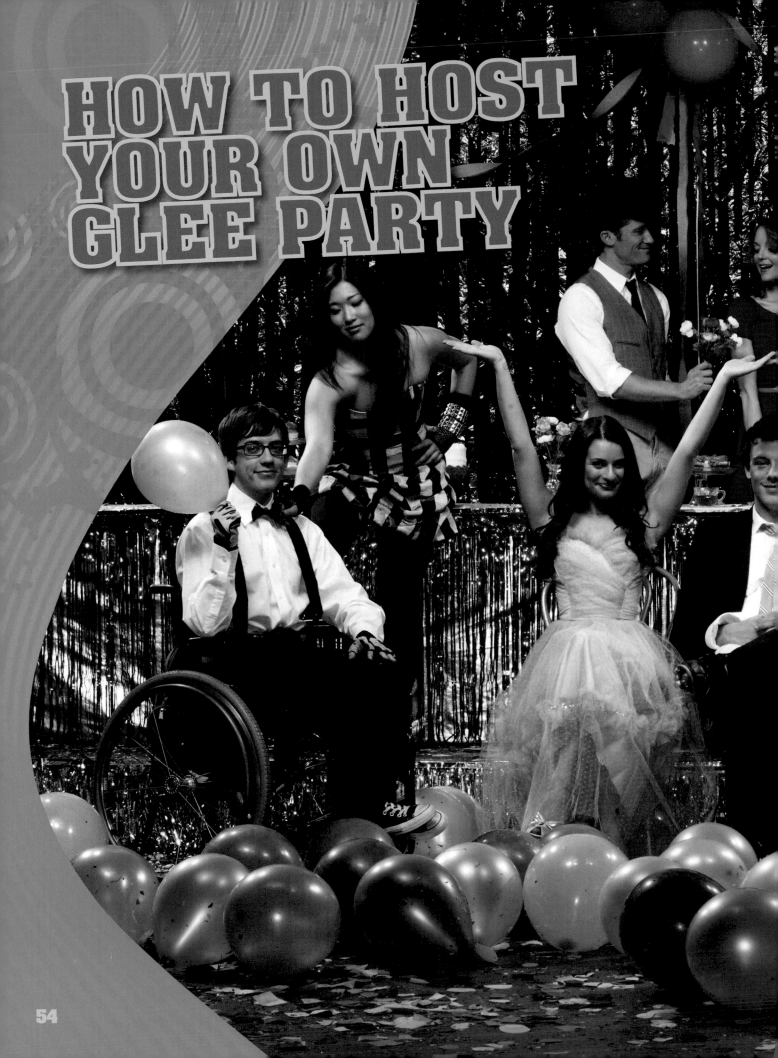

HOW TO HOST YOUR OWN GLEE PARTY

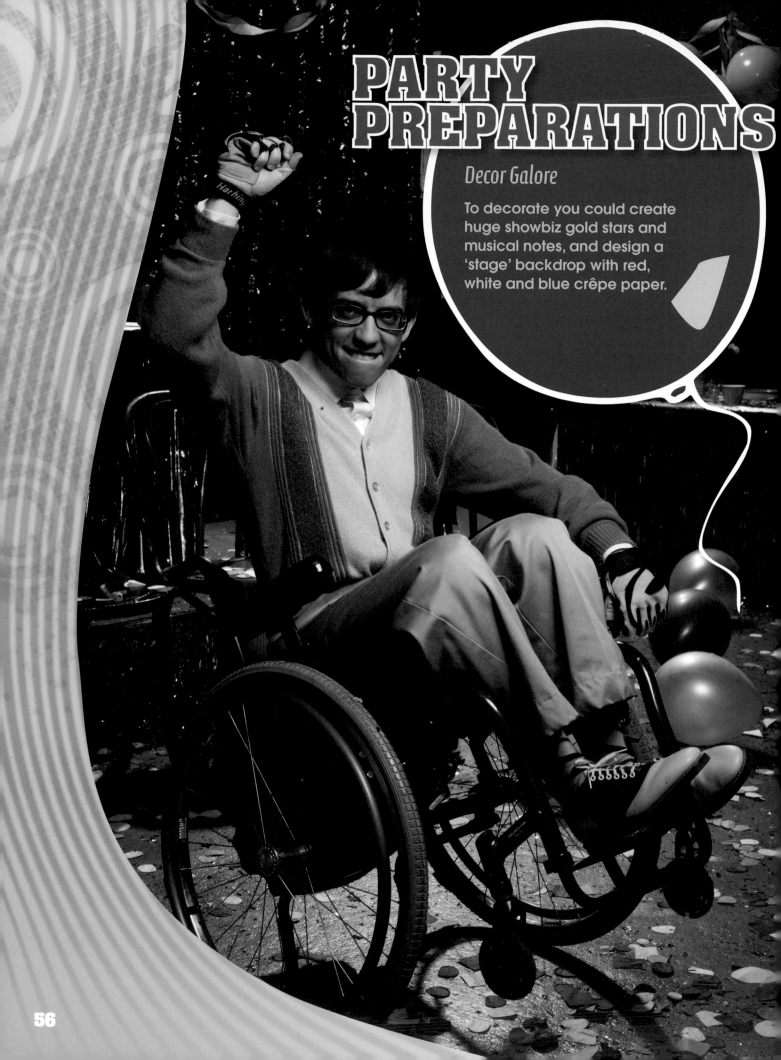

PARTY PREPARATIONS

Decor Galore

To decorate you could create huge showbiz gold stars and musical notes, and design a 'stage' backdrop with red, white and blue crêpe paper.

Class Wars

When you send out the invites divide your group of friends into groups: The Jocks, The Teachers and The Geeks and tell them to dress up accordingly. Or split your friends into song groups and challenge them to recreate Kurt's 'Single Ladies' routine or the Gleester's best costumed moment.

Perfect Props

Splash out on some comedy wigs and face paints to create your very own rock 'n' roll moment. Have rosettes and plastic toy trophies for prizes and ask everyone to bring a hairbrush for singing.

SNACKS

Cheerleader's cheese and pineapple

New Directions Selections: Opt for pick 'n' mix or yummy savoury snacks.

Shue's sausages on a stick

Brittany's ring doughnuts – there's nothing but air in the middle

Artie's wagon wheels

Puck's pizza

DESSERTS

Rachel's berry cheesecake
Santana's banana splits

BEVERAGES

Lush slush: No Glee party would be complete without some ice-cold syrupy frozen drink to leave everyone quaking with fear. Crush up a glass full of ice and add lemonade and blue, pink or yellow food colouring. *Voilà*! Your very own beverage of terror.

Sour Sue's lemon quenchers: made from cordial, garnished with lemon slices and very bitter.

Emma's OCD grapes: with a sign telling you to ask for permission before you touch.

PARTY GAMES

Go Global

Get a video camera ready for your very own You Tube moment. Break out your best Shue dance moves or blast out a power ballad à la Miss Rachel Berry.

Channel Kurt

Homage the Hummel by asking everyone to bring a plain white tee which you can design with fabric paints, pens, sequins and stars. Then hold your own runway show.

Pin the...

Accessory on Kurt or glasses on Artie.

Dance Off

Choose a special song that's in the charts and challenge groups of three or four to go off and make up a dance routine in fifteen minutes.

Play Musical Charades

As one friend attempts to mime a song title everyone else has to sing their guesses.

Pass the Parcel

Create a special parcel including the best quotes from Glee and a sweet under each layer. When the music stops whoever is holding the parcel has to read their quote in the voice of the character and then they can scoff their goodie.

glee EPISODE 10
HAIROGRAPHY

If Will thought Sue had stopped meddling with Glee Club he will be sorely disappointed. The McKinley High Queen of Mean is back and this time she wants the Glee Club's set list. In fact, as the school's 'fine arts administrator', she is demanding it. Will knows she's up to no good. His suspicions are only confirmed when he catches Brittany recording rehearsals on her mobile phone. 'Coach Sylvester didn't tell me to do this,' she blurts out. When Sue asks him to remind her of the names and postcodes of the other two schools competing at Sectionals the penny finally drops. Sue is going to leak his set list.

On Emma's advice Will decides to travel to the other schools to find out what is going on. His first stop is the Jane Adams Academy, a reform school for juvenile delinquent girls. After making his way through the prison-like security Will meets Grace Hitchens and explains his concerns. Grace is affronted. 'You think that because our students are thieves and arsonists, that we're cheaters too?' she barks. Erm, yes?

Continuing his investigative work (or not) Will promptly offers to let Grace's girls use the McKinley High auditorium as they don't have one of their own. Um, nicely executed Detective Schue. When the Jane Adams posse duly turn up and sing and dance in front of New Directions they are surprisingly good. Pulling off a sexy hair-flicking, booty-shaking rendition of 'Bootylicious' the performance packs quite a punch. Will is worried. Grace's girls are stiff competition.

Rachel dismisses their show as 'hairography', explaining that the excessive barnet flicking is to hide other flaws. This makes Will decide that his Glee clubbers could benefit from some extra tresses of their own and duly presents them with an array of rather wild wigs. Still Schue clearly believes dressing up like a bad tribute band could give them the edge to secure their place in Sectionals.

In other news Quinn might be refusing to acknowledge Puck as her baby father but the mohawked lady killer is not about to give up and presents her with a parenting book he stole especially. Quinn is touched and wonders if things could be different if she gave Puck a chance to prove himself as a dad. She privately decides to give him a 'test drive' but realises she needs to find a way to distract Finn. Cornering Kurt she suggests he gives preppy Rachel a makeover to improve their chances at Sectionals. Kurt of course agrees.

Over at Rachel's he tells her that he wants every boy to do a double-take when she walks past. But there is only one boy, as Rachel confesses: 'I'm in love with Finn.' Suddenly all Kurt's wardrobe goodwill is out the window as jealousy sets in. He hatches a wicked plan. He tells Rachel that he knows Finn likes loose-looking ladies. A 'ho chic' makeover begins.

Meanwhile Terri's pregnancy ruse is getting harder and harder. Keen to distract Will she buys him a Blue Bomber – the car he drove when they dated at high school. She suggests that Will could do it up as a stress-relief project. But just as Terri thinks her plan is back on track she learns that Quinn has decided to keep her baby. She considers coming clean but Kendra talks her

out of it. The sneaky sister has a plan – she'll ask Quinn to babysit her three boys: 'Five minutes with those little mongrels and she'll have her tubes tied.'

Word has got out about the Jane Adams Academy's visit to McKinley High and Will receives a visit from the choir director of Haverbrook School for the Deaf. He thinks his kids should get to use the auditorium too. Will agrees.

Rachel arrives at school sporting her new sizzling look and Finn is spellbound. He readily agrees to go over to her house that evening to practise their hairography. With Finn distracted Quinn asks Puck if he'd like to help her babysit Kendra's kids.

On the Friday night Rachel is primed to seduce Finn with her new slutty look. She appears in a skintight, black catsuit and coated in make-up and begins a breathy performance of 'You're The One That I Want' from *Grease*. Finn finds it all very uncomfortable. So much so that he labels her 'a sad, clown hooker'. Ouch! Rachel is mortified as he explains that he was only telling Kurt last week how he likes natural-looking girls.

Round at Chez Brat, Quinn and Puck are tied to chairs by their young charges but manage to bring calm to the house with an acoustic version of 'Papa Don't Preach'. Kendra dubs Quinn 'an exorcist'. Satisfied with their night's work Puck declares that they can 'do this parenting thing'.

Back at school Rachel is on the warpath and accuses Kurt of trying to 'eliminate the competition'. After a heated exchange Kurt concedes that there is no hope of either of them bagging Finn: 'He loves Quinn and they're having a baby together.'

SONGS

'True Colors'
originally sung by *Cyndi Lauper*

'Bootylicious' originally sung by *Destiny's Child*

'Papa Don't Preach'
originally sung by *Madonna*

'You're The One That I Want'
from the muscial *Grease*

'Hair'/'Crazy In Love' from the musical *Hair*/originally sung by *Beyoncé*

'Imagine' originally sung by *John Lennon*

The Haverbrook kids have arrived at the school auditorium and watch bemused as New Directions' hairography performance – a mash-up of 'Crazy In Love' and 'Hair' – gets underway. When the deaf kids take to the stage the McKinley High pupils are immediately humbled by their simple hand-sign performance of 'Imagine'. One by one they join their rivals on the stage and sing along.

Just as Quinn is beginning to see a new side of Puck she is brought down to earth with a bump by Santana, Puck's on–off girlfriend. The latino cheerleader tells her to back off and reveals that Puck was 'sexting' her the entire babysitting night. When Puck doesn't deny the allegation Quinn's mind is made up. She will give Terri the baby. Terri is ecstatic with Quinn's change of heart. Quinn tells her that a girl needs a good father and that she will get that in Will. When the teacher arrives home he is surprised to get a hug from Quinn. He reveals he has sold the Blue Bomber to get a family-friendly car. Quinn heads off to find Finn and the two have a heart-to-heart in the school corridor declaring their love while a sad Rachel and Kurt look on.

A gracious Will tells Sue that she was right about his OTT plans for the club. From now on there will be 'no gimmicks and false theatricality'. He gives her the set list. Later in a meeting with the choir directors from the rival schools Sue persuades them to take the list of songs she's now holding in her cold, treacherous hands. She urges them to work with her to defeat New Directions.

Oh Sue, you double-crossing wrong-un.

I'm a sex shark.
If I stop moving, I die.

People call me a screw-up
because I think school's for
suckers, but I got ambition.

NOAH 'PUCK' PUCKERMAN

Age: 16

Puck has worked hard to be popular. A feared member of the McKinley football team he throws his weight around on and off the pitch.

The buff teenager is best known for bullying his fellow classmates into submission and for his relentless quest to love and leave the school's hottest chicks. Puck's pool-cleaning business has also led to the seduction of a string of neighbourhood MILFs only too keen to check out his perfect pecs.

However behind the bad boy rep and relentless libido is just a normal teenage boy dealing with his own insecurities.

Puck secretly pursues cougars as he got sick of young girls shooting him down and making him feel terrible about himself. Yet there is one high school girl Puck wants (and loves) – that's Quinn, but he knows she just sees him as a Lima loser. When he gets her pregnant he is determined to stand by her and be a better man than his own deadbeat father – even when he sees her passing off Finn as her baby's father.

Despite his constant womanising and 'geek dumpster tossing' Puck's time in Glee Club has given him a chance to really belong. He would never admit he cares but it is no coincidence that Puck is always the first in line to fiercely defend New Directions – whether it be slashing Vocal Adrenaline's tyres or threatening to rearrange Jessie's face when he wrongs Rachel.

Reacting with brute force might seem like the only way he knows how to express himself but there's hope for Puck. He's proven loyal to the people he loves and Mercedes and Quinn have both seen flashes of an inner nice guy just waiting to be tapped – if only he could get that wandering eye under control.

Love interests: Quinn, Santana, Brittany, Rachel, Mercedes

Rivals: Finn

Musical heroes: Journey, Kiss, Beck

FACT! Puck has a nipple ring because he's kinda rock 'n' roll

glee EPISODE 11
MATTRESS

It's yearbook photo time at McKinley High but New Directions are feeling far from Glee-ful. It's a truth universally acknowledged that the Glee Club photo is a magnet for ridicule and vandalism and to be honest no one really wants their photo featured apart from Rachel.

Even Principal Figgins appears only too happy to exclude New Directions. He agrees with Sue's verdict that it will only be subjecting 'the little freaks to more humiliation' plus he's using the space to sell advertising instead. But Will is adamant that the Glee Club should have its rightful place – so much so that he even agrees to fork out the $350 for space designated to a quarter-page ad. With the promise of money, Figgins agrees that the Glee Club will have its place but there will only be room for two team captains.

As Rachel is the only person who wants to be included – it's good practice for paparazzi posing in her future showbiz life – she gets a unanimous vote from the rest of the club. When no one else volunteers Will tells her to chose a co-captain. She eventually settles on Finn. Finn takes his responsibility with grace and even allows Rachel to teach him to smile correctly.

But in the locker room before the shoot he is pounced on by his fellow jocks who wage war on his face with a magic marker. When Finn is a no-show at the shoot Rachel is disappointed but carries on determinedly. She gets talking to the photographer Denis who reveals his next job is shooting and directing a TV ad for a local

mattress store. Rachel duly manages to persuade him to hire her and the rest of the Glee Club and rushes to tell the others who are sure this brush with fame will at last give them kudos at school.

On set at the mattress store the script is proving to be quite mediocre and lacks sparkle. Rachel suggests they do a song instead and the Gleesters pull off a blinding performance of 'Jump', leaping all over the store in blue pyjamas.

At home Will is hopping mad. Opening a drawer he stumbles across one of the pads Terri has been using to fake her pregnancy. He confronts a startled Terri in the kitchen and the whole sorry story comes out. Will can't believe what he is hearing and storms out. Devastated he makes his way to school where he finds a pile of twelve mattresses stacked up in the auditorium. He pulls one into his office, unwraps it and beds down for the night.

Fresh from another controversial rant on her TV segment, Sue's Corner, the cheerleading coach is interested to spot New Directions prancing around on a TV commercial. The next day she is amused to be approached by Quinn who asks to be allowed back in the cheerleading squad and also to be included in the yearbook photo. Sue refuses point blank and then informs her former protégée that as New Directions received the mattresses as payment for the advert they are no longer amateurs and have therefore disqualified themselves from Sectionals.

When Will is summoned to the principal's office he argues that the mattresses can be returned until Figgins points out that he's already opened and slept on one. Looks like Glee Club is over – again. But the dastardly cheerleading coach wasn't wrong when she told Quinn she reminded her of a young Sue Sylvester. Behind Quinn's angelic face is a steely determination. Approaching the jubilant teacher in her office she reminds her of all the free shoes, tanning sessions and haircuts the squad have snagged over the past few months and the recriminations if they were revealed. As Sue seethes, Quinn reveals the terms that will buy her silence: a full-page Glee photo in the yearbook paid for by Sue and her place back on the squad. A pained Sue nods and Quinn goes on her way, pausing for a second to tell the coach she's changed her mind. Stuff her place on the team, she'll stick with Glee – a club that's proud to have her.

A disheartened Will may have hit rock bottom after the discovery that he is not a dad-to-be and the mattress debacle but at least he's found a solution to get the kids to Sectionals. Seeing as he was the only one who opened the mattress, and so accepting payment, New Directions can still compete – but without him. The kids are unsure about going it alone but Will says they'll be just fine and urges them to hold their heads up high for their Glee yearbook piccy.

New Directions take his advice, crooning along to 'Smile' as they strike a pose. Of course it's no time at all before their photo is *hilariously* defaced with predictable captions such as 'Lame', 'Losers' and 'No Direction' but hey, what do those punks know anyway?

SONGS

'Smile' originally sung by *Lily Alllen*

'Jump' originally sung by *Van Halen*

'Smile' originally sung by *Michael Jackson*

'When You're Smiling' originally sung by *Louis Armstrong*

'You guys, I want us to always remember this moment. Soon, there may be agents and managers and movie deals, but right now I want us to remember what it feels like to be here together as a team.' *Rachel*

glee EPISODE 12
SECTIONALS

Rachel has a hunch that there is something going on with Puck and Quinn. Seeing as all the other Gleesters appear to have worked that one out already (but are keeping schtum) we don't rate Rachel's chance of being the next Jessica Fletcher any time soon. But she's still pretty crafty and slyly told Quinn about a test for a rogue gene only carried by Jewish people. So, when she saw non-Jew Quinn talking to non-Jew Finn about needing a test then the last piece of the daddy jigsaw fell into place – and produced a picture of Puck.

With poor Will *persona non grata* when it comes to the Sectionals, Emma steps in to help. Agreeing to accompany the kids, *on her wedding day*. We've heard of reluctant brides but quite frankly this is ridiculous. Her husband-to-be Ken has agreed to postpone the nuptials for a few hours so she can help Will out but it doesn't look like he's particularly thrilled either.

The Glee clubbers have to decide their own set list and eventually settle on 'Proud Mary' and 'Don't Stop Believin''. Mercedes asks to sing the ballad and demonstrates her talent with a blinding performance of 'And I Am Telling You' from *Dreamgirls*. Everyone agrees she should take centre stage, even – shock, horror – Rachel. After this first act of kindness Rachel's benevolence isn't complete. Next she opts for the 'cruel to be kind' variety. She has something to tell Finn...

Well, what do you know? Next thing Finn is serving Puck a knuckle sandwich as the pair of them wrestle on the floor. Looks like that cat is well and truly out of the bag. A horrified Will quickly breaks them up.

Finn demands to know the truth from Quinn who finally comes clean. Finn storms off leaving everyone shell-shocked and Rachel sobbing at the trouble she's caused. She apologises to Quinn who is philosophical – after all Rachel did the one thing she was too frightened to do. Puck says he wants to be a good father but Quinn announces that she wants to 'do this on my own'.

It's time to head to Sectionals. Finn is nowhere to be seen but that's the least of New Directions' problems. They are performing last, after the Jane Adams Academy and Haverbrook and there is something very familiar about their set lists – the Jane Adams girls pull off a hair-flicking showstopper to 'And I Am Telling You', swiftly followed by a wheelchair-bound spectacular to 'Proud Mary'. Next up the deaf kids sign their way through 'Don't Stop Believin'' leaving New Directions aghast.

Emma makes an emergency call to Will. He immediately confronts Sue who denies she leaked the list but taunts him that soon Glee will be history with Figgins' funding bankrolling into the cheer squad's budget instead.

Will thinks she's despicable but time is of the essence and he rushes off to find Finn.

In the locker room he tells the teenager that New Directions are in dire straits and can't win without him. Finn questions why things can't just go back to the way they were. Will tells him you can't always get what you want. Then he leaves his car keys next to Finn.

Meanwhile Emma corners the two rival show choir directors and berates them for cheating. At the same time

SONGS

'And I Am Telling You I'm Not Going' from the musical *Dreamgirls*

'Don't Rain On My Parade' from the muscial *Funny Girl*

'You Can't Always Get What You Want' originally sung by *The Rolling Stones*

'Somebody To Love' originally sung by *Queen*

'My Life Would Suck Without You' originally sung by *Kelly Clarkson*

Rachel is rounding up the troops. They need new songs fast and she asks Mercedes if she has anything else to offer. Mercedes admits there is little else in her repertoire but perhaps Rachel can sing. It turns out La Berry does have a little something up her sleeve and the group settle on 'Somebody To Love' as their closing number. But time is running out and they need a third song. Suddenly Finn walks in with some sheet music. Hope is restored!

New Directions take to the stage where Rachel pulls off a blinder, earning a standing ovation for her tremendous performance of 'Don't Rain On My Parade'. Next the Glee clubbers take on Finn's song 'You Can't Always Get What You Want', belting it out with gusto and to rapturous applause. As Emma plays the performance down the phone to Will, he weeps with emotion. 'Somebody To Love' provides them with a hat-trick of crowd pleasers. Everyone is overjoyed. As the three judges deliberate their fate Grace admits she cheated and offers to own up but it's too late – the winning show choir has been selected.

As Will gets ready for Emma and Ken's wedding, Terri returns home and tries to make amends. She says she's

seeing a therapist but Will says he no longer cares for her. Arriving at the legion hall he finds Emma alone. Ken jilted her after she postponed the wedding. She admits that she has fallen for Will and it's too difficult to be around him so she's handed in her notice. Will informs her that he's just left his wife but Emma apologises and says she still needs to leave. Nooooo.

Back at school on Monday, Will and Sue are involved in a showdown about Sectionals in Figgins' office. The evidence against Sue is damning as the rival Glee coaches have 'fessed up. An angry Figgins dismisses her from coaching the squad and suspends her from teaching at McKinley. And Will is back directing Glee! Sue takes her punishment but not before squaring up to Will and promising revenge: 'You're about to board the Sue Sylvester Express. Destination horror!'

In the auditorium the kids have a surprise for Will. Handing him the huge trophy they won at Sectionals they serenade him with 'My Life Would Suck Without You.' Aw. But there is one more prize Will needs to bag. Rushing along the corridor he finds Emma on her way out of school with the last of her belongings. He leans in and kisses her.

'Ladies and gentlemen, New Directions.' *Rachel*

ARTIE ABRAMS

Age: 16

Artie is the wheelchair-bound geek who dreams of being a dancer.

Bespectacled Artie has been confined to a chair since the age of eight when he was in a bad car crash with his mother. Although his mom walked away from the crash, the damage to Artie's spinal cord was irreversible and he was left paralysed from the waist down.

Despite having been this way ever since, Artie still struggles to accept his fate.

As he says himself, 'I do a pretty good job of being in denial about the hopelessness of my condition.'

This is definitely the case when Artie starts to dream about owning tap shoes and dancing his way through a musical number. As he admits to Tina, thinking too hard about his situation freaks him out but deep down he knows his legs will never work again.

Proud and independent, Artie often gets frustrated with his chair. He also doesn't like people feeling sorry for him and often feels like his chair stops him from being normal. He finds it upsetting when his peers don't treat him as an equal and was left quietly offended when his fellow Gleesters dismissed his need for transport to Sectionals so easily.

Artie has a good heart and is happy to make sacrifices for the greater good – like donating the money for the minibus to pay for disability ramps.

Before Glee Club Artie often got mocked by the jocks and cool kids but now he has allies – not least Tina who he is really beginning to fall for.

At times he can be moody and lash out but he is also straight talking, sensitive and is not afraid to apologise when he's in the wrong – like the time he realises he has been objectifying Tina. Now they are well on their way to becoming Glee's hottest couple.

Although Artie will always secretly long for a magic fix, he's come to realise he has to make the best of what he's got. He loves singing and dancing – even if it is on two wheels.

Love interests: Tina

Rivals: The football team

Musical heroes: KISS, Men Without Hats

FACT! Artie writes Def Poetry Jams

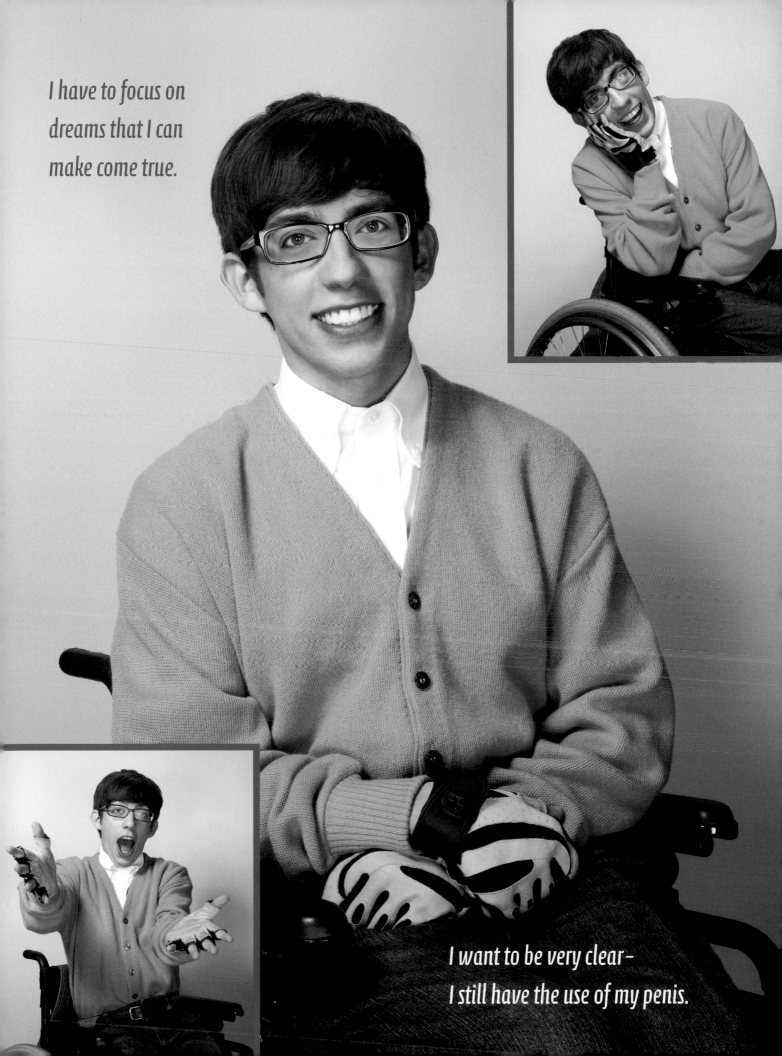

I have to focus on dreams that I can make come true.

I want to be very clear – I still have the use of my penis.

glee EPISODE 13
HELL-O

So surely winning Sectionals gives New Directions school kudos right? Rachel thinks so, but a cup of frozen drink to the face would suggest differently.

With Quinn and Finn like totally over, Rachel has snagged the hot jock and is already printing out love calendars. Understandably Finn is feeling pressurised (and he still misses Quinn). The pregnant cheerleader is hardly smitten with Puck, her baby father either – especially when he tells her he doesn't dig fat chicks…

When Figgins moves the goal posts again Will is faced with two nasty surprises: Glee Club funding will only continue if the kids place at Regionals and from now on they'll be sharing the auditorium with the cheer squad. As Will takes in this news a jubilant tracksuit-clad figure appears behind him. How on earth did Sue get her job back? It appears she's back on the blackmail trail again, having forced Figgins to reinstate her thanks to incriminating pictures involving whipped cream.

This week's assignment is songs that have 'hello' in the title. Will thinks Finn needs to find the rock star within, so Finn has belted out an awesome performance of 'Hello, I Love You' for his. Afterwards, prompted by Sue's latest attempt to sabotage Glee Club by splitting up Rachel and Finn, Brittany and Santana decide to make a move on him. Smiling suggestively they offer to go on a date with him together. Finn can't believe his luck.

When Rachel gets heavy again Finn bites the bullet and informs her that he's not on the market for a girlfriend right now. He needs to connect with his inner rock star. A tearful Rachel tells him he is only acting this way because Quinn humiliated him and he's worried about his reputation. Later when she spots him flirting with Brittany and Santana at

SONGS

'Hello, I Love You'
originally sung by *The Doors*

'Gives You Hell'
originally sung by *All-American Rejects*

'Highway To Hell' originally sung by *AC/DC*

'Hello' originally sung by *Lionel Richie*

'Hello Again' originally sung by *Neil Diamond*

'Hello Goodbye' originally sung by *The Beatles*

Glee rehearsals she immediately volunteers to sing. Pointedly she has omitted the 'o' from Will's 'hello' brief, blasting out 'Gives You Hell' in a terrified Finn's direction.

When Rachel has a chance encounter with Vocal Adrenaline's hunky star singer Jessie St James in a local music store, she is pretty gobsmacked to learn that Jessie knows her name. He says he saw her performance at Sectionals and while she lacked the 'emotional depth' of Barbra Streisand he thinks she's talented. Jessie coolly suggests Rachel joins him in a piano-accompanied duet of 'Hello' and then he asks her out!

Unfortunately Finn is not having nearly as much fun on his date with Brittany and Santana. The two cheerleaders are behaving obnoxiously and wittering on about the hottest guys in school. It is only after they discuss Finn and remark that his 'dwarf girlfriend is dragging down his rep' that he pipes up from across the table reminding them he's still there. Santana informs him that she and Brittany provide the best dates ever – usually concluding with the two of them making out together in return for being bought dinner. Finn looks intrigued by this until Santana resumes the Rachel bashing. Giving up hope he slopes off home.

Will's decided he and Emma need to start from the beginning with a date, so he's invited her over to his place to cook for her. All is going well, and they have a little smooch to 'Hello Again', which Will dedicates to her as 'their song'. But as things heat up on the sofa Emma freaks out. She confesses she's a virgin. Gentlemanly Will tells her it's fine and suggests they watch a film instead.

What's this? Finn wants Rachel back? Well it's too late, Miss Berry is smitten with her new beau Jessie. Finn thinks Jessie's interest in Rachel is suspicious and grasses her up to Mr Schue. Will decides to pay their steely vocal coach, Shelby Corcoran, a visit. He explains he is worried about Rachel fraternising with the enemy, but Shelby is unconcerned. 'The heart wants what the heart wants,' she says. Well, the next thing we know the two vocal coaches are indulging in some frenzied tonsil tennis in Will's apartment. As things get racy Will is hesitant. He confesses to Shelby that he only separated from his wife a few weeks before and that he has just started seeing someone new.

New Directions think Rachel needs an intervention. Convinced Jessie is spying on them they warn her it's Jessie or Glee. Who will she chose? Good job Aunty Sue is on hand to help her. Gathered in her office are McKinley High's Old Maids Club. They are there to warn her about the dangers of putting career before love. Doubt has set in for Rachel so she goes to Carmel High to find Jessie. She warns that if he's playing her it will be the sort of heartbreak she's likely to hold on to for the rest of her life. Jessie decides that although Rachel's met the star of Vocal Adrenaline, now it's time to meet the real him: 'The guy who is nuts about you.' Smooth. But why is Jessie exchanging knowing looks with Shelby behind Rachel's back?

Emma is busy planning a surprise dinner at Will's house when who should turn up but Terri. Awkward? Terri spots a copy of *The Jazz Singer* soundtrack and takes great pleasure in telling Emma that 'Hello Again' was her and Will's prom song. The next day, Emma confronts Will with the 1993 Yearbook. She thinks subconsciously Will isn't ready to move on and he should have some time alone.

Meanwhile Rachel lies to Finn claiming she has finished with Jessie. Finn thinks they should be together but Rachel tells him it's too close to Regionals to get distracted. But that doesn't stop Finn giving Rachel lovelorn looks all through their rehearsals of 'Hello Goodbye'. Looks like those rock-star days are over, Finn?

SANTANA LOPEZ

Age: 16

Santana is a boy-crazy cheerleader who originally joined Glee Club to spy for Coach Sylvester. Seductive and predatory, Santana uses her substantial sexual power to manipulate people into doing what she wants. She is bitchy and feisty and the Queen of Mean.

Her alpha female tendencies mean she likes to be the centre of attention and will try to crush any rival who pays her on–off booty call Puck attention. Santana isn't sure she really wants him but enjoys keeping him dangling as her back-up boy. When Quinn and Mercedes express an interest in him she reacts venomously marking her territory.

Although she signed up for celibacy club Santana is a sexual predator. She loves no-strings sex and was quite happy to take Finn's virginity then head off for a burger.

Santana's best friend is Brittany who she sometimes makes out with to get boys to buy them dinner. Brittany has inferred that they've slept together too although Santana seems reluctant to talk about that.

Ruthless and ambitious, Santana has her sights set on bagging the chief cheerleading role. Although Quinn is her friend she is pleased by her fall from grace as it means she has a shot of being Queen of the cheerleading team.

Although Santana acts indifferently about Glee Club she clearly enjoys singing and dancing with New Directions.

As she eventually admits, 'No one's forcing me to be here. And if you ever tell anyone this I'll deny it – but I like being in Glee Club. It's the best part of my day, OK?'

Love interests: Puck, Finn

Rivals: Quinn, Mercedes, Rachel, womankind

Musical heroes: Madonna, Lady Gaga

FACT! Santana considers herself to be smokin' hot at sexting

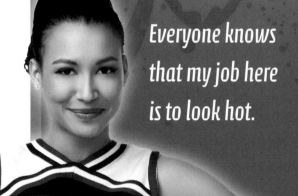

Everyone knows that my job here is to look hot.

SANTANA'S GUIDE TO HOT DATING

Santana knows her job is to look hot and now that Quinn is no longer the queen, there's plenty of reasons why she is now the top dog.

She knows the rules...
'Sex is not dating.'

...but she's prepared to experiment
'You buy us dinner and we make out in front of you. It's like the best deal ever.'

She can see an opportunity...
'...it's high time you lost the big V – everything about you screams virgin. You're about as sexy as a Cabbage Patch Kid. It's exhausting to look at you.' (Finn)

...and she also knows when to quit
'Your credit score is terrible.' (Puck)

She's got experience...
'I've noticed that it takes about 20 or so times before the feeling of accomplishment really kicks in.'

...and she's prepared to share it
'I need a younger, inferior man.'

She knows when to chat...
'My sexts are too hot to erase.'

...and when to keep quiet
'I don't talk during.'

She's knows what's good for her image...
'So come on, let's do the deed. It'll be great for my image, and Sue will promote me to head cheerleader. It's win–win.' (Finn)

...and for his too
'I mean, if he were dating, say, popular girls like us, he would go from dumpy to smokin.' (Finn)

BRIT'S GUIDE TO BEING A DIM-WIT

Life in general...

I don't know how to turn on a computer.

Sometimes I forget my middle name.

Mr Schuester: Who can tell me what a ballad is?
Brittany: A male duck.

I'm pretty sure my cat's been reading my diary.

Did you know that dolphins are just gay sharks?

On love, sex, and why you should never let her cook you dinner...

Kissing my armpit is a really big turn on for me.

I don't know why I only made fourth on the Glist, I made out with like everyone in the school, girls, boys, Mr Kidney the janitor. I need to do something to get into the top three.

Santana: Sex is not dating.
Brittany: If it were, Santana and I would be dating.

(To Kurt) So, you're pretty much the only guy in this school that I haven't made out with, because I thought you were capital-G gay, but now that you're not, having a perfect record would mean a lot to me. So, let me know if you want to tap this.

It's just that most of us don't know how to bake. I find recipes confusing.

Sometimes I add a teaspoon of sand.

On health...

When I pulled my hamstring I went to a misogynist.

I've been here since first period. I had a cold and I took all my antibiotics at the same time, and now I can't remember how to leave.

Artie: I'm kinda getting cold feet.
Brittany: Can you even feel your feet?

The trials and tribulations of being in Glee Club...

There are so many lyrics.

Will Schuester: Take it away, Brittany.
Brittany: Take what away?

So, Hairography. It works best when you pretend like you're getting tasered. So you just move your head around and pretend like you're spazzing and stuff.

You guys, it's like cool epilepsy.

On self-confidence...

You look terrible. I look awesome.

Rachel: Where's Quinn?
Brittany: Probably down at the mall looking for elastic-waist pants.

I didn't wear a bra, and I had them turn on the air conditioning.

BRITTANY PIERCE

I just don't understand anything.

Age: 16

Brittany is a simple but happy soul whose one goal in life is to make out with every guy at McKinley High.

No matter what situation is unfolding the Glee-Clubbing cheerleader is firmly in her own little world but despite her low IQ, Brittany comes alive when she is singing and dancing.

Her best friend is Santana who she follows around and parrots whenever an opinion is required. Generally Brittany will do what anyone tells her – hence why Coach Sylvester is always using her to spy.

Like Santana, Brittany has no qualms about sleeping her way around high school. She will put out for anyone and is one of many notches on Puck's bed post. She also implies she's slept with Santana, and when Kurt decides to go straight in an effort to bond with his dad, Brittany sets her sights on him

Love interests: Kurt, Finn, Puck

Rivals: Rachel

Musical heroes: Lady Gaga

FACT! Brittany thinks her cat reads her diary

'I'm reasonably confident that you will be adding revenge to the long list of things you're no good at, right next to being married, running a high school glee club, and finding a hair style that doesn't make you look like a lesbian...'

'You know what else I'm gonna bring? I'm gonna bring some Asian cookery to wipe your head with. Cause right now you've got enough product in your hair to season a wok.'

'Hey buddy, get a haircut? Looks awful.'

SUE VERSUS WILL'S HAIR

'Oh, hey William. I thought I smelled cookies wafting from the ovens of the little elves who live in your hair...'

'Your hair looks so much like a briar patch that I'm expecting racist, animated Disney characters to pop out and start singing about living on the bayou...'

'Wow, I just lost my train of thought. You have so much margarine in your hair...'

'Nobody quite like the Material Girl to empower my Cheerios. Just like your hairdresser's empowered you to look absolutely ridiculous...'

'I've proven that I can wipe you and your Glee Club off the face of the Earth. But what kind of a world would that be, Will? A world where I couldn't constantly ridicule your hair.'

'You wouldn't even know if your Glee Club was using your office to breed rabbits for pets or for food. You know why? You're too busy chasing tail and loading your hair with enormous amounts of product. I mean today it just looks like you put lard in it.'

'I don't trust a man with curly hair. I can't help picturing small birds laying sulphurous eggs in there, and I find it disgusting.'

'I was down at the pharmacy today, and they're having a monster sale on Dep. Dep is a hair gel. And once again, I am making fun of your incredibly stupid hairdo.'

'And here's the truth. I mercilessly pick on Will Shuester's lustrous, wavy hair because I am jealous. There I said it.'

THE POWER OF MADONNA

Oh that pesky Sue, the blackmail continues. Armed with the incriminating photos of Figgins in her bed Sue has a new demand. This time she wants Madonna's greatest hits played on loop over the school PA. The cheerleading coach reveals that she's always wanted to play homage to the pop icon responsible for her 'take-no-prisoners demeanour'. Knowing the alternative is ritual humiliation Figgins reluctantly agrees.

Meanwhile Rachel is looking for advice. Say you were dating a boy who wanted to do 'it'. What would Quinn, Santana and Brittany do? Not that she's dating a boy. No senior boy got worked up in her bedroom last night, then went all crabby when she said no and refused to take the Care Bear she won for him home. No, Rachel's talking hypothetically of course. 'Never-says-no' Santana shrugs. Overhearing, Will is less than impressed. He advises the girls to talk to Emma. Rachel reveals she already tried that but, asking Miss Pillsbury for advice on sex is, well, just a little bit futile.

Turns out Rachel isn't the only one who's been getting short shrift from a boy recently. Artie may have forgiven Tina for lying about her stutter but he's been pretty arrogant of late telling her to ditch the goth look and wear tighter clothes. His suggestion that she needs to 'work it more' if she wants them to be an item has left Tina stunned.

Later Will tells Emma that he wants to help empower the girls of McKinley to hold their own. So after vowing to be the saviour of schoolgirls everywhere Will happens to catch a glimpse of Sue's cheer squad rehearsing 'Ray Of Light'. Sue naturally isn't impressed with their stellar performance, declaring that somewhere in an English stately home, 'Madonna is weeping,' but Will is inspired: the Material Girl will be that week's Glee Club theme.

Rachel and Kurt are ecstatic but Finn and Puck are unsure. Madonna may be one super hot chick but her songs are not very manly. But Schue thinks it's high time the Glee guys had a lesson in respect. 'You're disrespectful, bullying, sexist and, I hate to say it, misogynistic,' he announces. 'Madonna's message is about equality and that's something the guys can learn from her music.'

Having seen Santana wearing a wristband inscribed with 'WWMD' – What Would Madonna Do? – Sue believes Madonna would tell her squad to bag themselves younger men. But while Brittany is busy dating a seven-year-old, Santana is yet to snare a 'younger inferior man'. She finally settles on Finn, who according to Brittany, is three days younger. Locking in on her target a sultry Santana approaches Finn and offers to help him lose the Big V. He's unsure at first but eventually agrees.

As Madonna filters through the corridors and classrooms of McKinley High one room is painfully silent. Emma wants to know why her office has been overlooked and Sue is only too happy to set her straight. 'You don't deserve the power of Madonna,' she explains. 'You have all the sensuality of one of those pandas down at the zoo who refused to mate.'

When Will ridicules Sue's hair it's not pretty. Suddenly a psycho Sylvester is flailing through the corridors taking out any unfortunate pupils who get in her way. Intrigued by this apparent hair complex, Kurt and Mercedes approach Coach Sylvester in her office. Dropping her guard she reveals how as a child she bleached her hair with household chemicals to recreate Madonna's look on the *True Blue* album. Kurt and Mercedes have a solution. They want Sue and her cheerleaders to star as Madonna for their multi-media video project, which turns out to be a visual feast as Sue 'vogues' her way through a stunning Madonna tribute even adding in her own special line: 'Will Schuester, I hate you.'

During a clandestine meeting in the library Jessie apologises to Rachel for his ungentlemanly behaviour. He says she deserves 'epic romance' while all the while giving her the St James smoulder. Rachel is like putty in his hands. 'I'm ready!' she squeals. Are you sure Rachel?

So Finn wants to do it, so does Rachel, and now – making it a trio of first-timers – Emma wants in on the cherry-popping action too, telling Will their own personal adventure will begin at 7.30pm that night at his apartment.

That night Operation Lose It is underway, Rachel, Finn and Emma prepare to be deflowered but will any of them actually go through with it? Although Rachel later claims to Finn she's done the deed, we know she's lying. Finn meanwhile is feeling guilty that he *did* do it so fibs and claims he didn't. Confusing? Just a bit. Then there's Emma, who like Rachel, couldn't go through with it. The next day in Will's office she apologises profusely. Will doesn't mind but thinks counselling could help her.

Will is surprised by his next visitor – Jessie St James. He wants to transfer to McKinley to join Glee and be with Rachel. Rachel is jubilant but everyone else is appalled. They already have to fight hard enough to get solos. Now with Jessie around there'll be even fewer opportunities. But hey, it's OK divas, Sue has the solution. A pair of singing cheerleaders would be yet another jewel in the Coach Sylvester crown to win Nationals (not to mention narking one Will Schuester off royally).

She duly enlists Mercedes and Kurt, which has the desired effect on Will. But as Kurt reasons: 'We love being in Glee, but being in the Cheerios will give us more opportunities to shine. We're doing both.'

Determined to make up for their misogyny the Glee guys finally relent and croon, 'What It Feels Like For A Girl'. Artie appears to be the most repentant apologising to Tina for objectifying her. After giving him one hell of a verbal dressing down Tina accepts his apology and they kiss.

SONGS

'**Express Yourself**'
originally sung by *Madonna*

'**Borderline/Open Your Heart**'
originally sung by *Madonna*

'**Like A Prayer**' originally sung by *Madonna*

'**Vogue**' originally sung by *Madonna*

'**Like A Virgin**' originally sung by *Madonna*

'**4 Minutes**' originally sung by *Madonna*

'**What It Feels Like For A Girl**'
originally sung by *Madonna*

THE RACHEL BERRY GUIDE TO MOTIVATION

 You might laugh because every time I sign my name I put a gold star after it. But it's a metaphor. And metaphors are important. My gold stars are a metaphor for me being a star.

If there's anything I've learned in my 16 years on the stage, it's that stars are rare, and when they're found, you have to let them shine.

 I try to post a MySpace video every day just to keep my talent alive and growing. Nowadays, being anonymous is worse than being poor. Fame is the most important thing in our culture now. And if there's one thing I've learned, it's that no one's just gonna hand it to you.

 Oh, we all have pressures, but you know how I deal with it? The natural way, with a rigorous diet and exercise routine. I'm up at 6:00 a.m. Every day. I have my protein shake with banana and flaxseed oil, and by 6:10, I'm on the elliptical. You know how I motivate myself? Not with anything artificial. I set a goal and I won't rest until I reach it.

I am really stressed out. But that's the price you pay for being a star.

 Look, I know who I am, OK? I know I can be a little abrasive, bossy and conceited... I know it sounds awful, but I'm the best one in there. I try the hardest, and I want it the most.

It's all about winning.

Everybody hates me. You think Glee Club is gonna change that? Being great at something is going to change it. Being a part of something special makes you special.

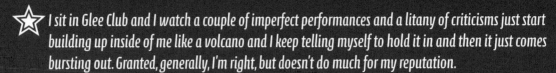 I sit in Glee Club and I watch a couple of imperfect performances and a litany of criticisms just start building up inside of me like a volcano and I keep telling myself to hold it in and then it just comes bursting out. Granted, generally, I'm right, but doesn't do much for my reputation.

I get caught up in the competitive hysteria, too. My goals are too selfish. You know, it's time for me to stop competing against everyone and start competing alongside them.

I have this pathological need to be popular, OK? I just want people to think I'm cool so bad sometimes that it just clouds my judgment.

When Barbra was a young ingénue, everyone told her in order to be a star, she'd have to get a nose job. Thankfully, she refused… We're gonna win because we're different. And that's what makes us special.

Just because I'm not good at anything other than singing doesn't mean I'm not any good if I can't sing.

 [To the Glee clubbers] I realized being a star didn't make me feel as special as being your friend. If I'd let you down when you needed me the most, I'd never forgive myself.

WILL SCHUESTER

Age: Mid 30s

As a former member of McKinley High's 1993 award-winning Glee Club, Will Schuester knows only too well what it is like to live and breathe show choir.

Scooping the Nationals title with a funky disco performance of 'That's The Way I Like It' was the highlight of Will's teenage years and he's not sure he's ever felt happier or more alive than in that moment.

Now as he guides a bunch of talented misfit kids through their own journey to Sectionals, Regionals and possibly Nationals he is every bit as passionate.

Will is the school's Spanish teacher but took over the direction of Glee Club after former coach Sandy was kicked out over allegations of indecent conduct with a pupil.

He puts his heart and soul into New Directions, caring deeply about the kids' welfare and fighting cheerleading coach Sue Sylvester tooth and nail to protect them.

His sensitive and caring attitude towards his pupils often results in him being a shoulder to cry on or the unwitting target of a heavy schoolgirl crush.

Will has only had one girlfriend, his high school sweetheart Terri, who he went on to wed, but is now free again after their break-up. His mind is in turmoil and it doesn't help that he works with sweet and kind (if a little crazy) guidance counsellor Emma Pillsbury who has a bad dose of love.

When Terri makes a mockery of their marriage by faking a pregnancy the deception hurts Will deeply and he is unable to move on instantly from it. He files for divorce and tries to make a fresh start with Emma but being newly single is a challenge. Will likes Emma but is easily distracted, also falling for the charms of rival show choir coach Shelby. It's clear he needed to be on his own for a while but now things are back on track with Emma, the lady it is clear he loves.

As his school life and personal life fall apart there are times when an emotional Will feels like everything is getting too much for him. He knows he sometimes makes bad decisions like pushing Sue to breaking point by pretending to seduce her but he isn't afraid to learn a lesson or say sorry.

Whatever difficulties come his way Will somehow finds the solution and is quick to bounce back. His pupils love and respect him with Finn even dubbing him a father figure. But the truth is it's a two-way relationship. Will loves working with New Directions and would be lost without them.

Love interests: Terri, Emma, April, Shelby

Rivals: Sue, Shelby, Ken, Bryan Ryan

Musical heroes: Justin Timberlake, Parliament, Young MC

FACT! Will has a degree in accounting

Glee Club –
it's where I belong.

I think, in all of this
'discovering who I
am' business, I took a
couple of wrong turns.

QUIZ
WHO IS YOUR GLEE BESTIE?

1 You've known each other since kindergarten but on the first day of high school how does she treat you?

A You don't see her for dust. She's too busy signing up for every drama and music activity available

B When a kid accidentally bangs into you she shouts at them down the corridor

C It's funny you never noticed she had a stutter before

D She passes you a diet plan – you'll only be mates if you make the cheerleading squad

2 What is your style?

A Preppy and virginal with cute twin sets

B Diva. Beyoncé has nothing on you

C You're rocking the punk goth look

D Never seen without your cheerleading outfit

3 How do you spend your evenings?

A Practising your singing and uploading videos to You Tube

B Perfecting your diva strut and watching Dreamgirls

C Listening to obscure emo bands in your bedroom

D Organising Celibacy Club of course

4 OMG! You're the victim of a frozen drink attack in the corridor. What does your bestie do?

A Hands you a tissue and says that one day suffering for your art will be worth it

B Quotes you an empowering line from a Jennifer Hudson song

C Looks at you utterly mortified

D Tells you your friendship is like soooo over, well at least in public anyway

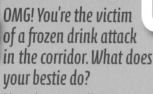

5 You confess you like a boy, what does your friend do?

A She tells you to cut out a pic of his face, stick it next to yours on a photo and visualise

B Warns you to stick with your own. Geeks don't bag jocks. Period

C Informs you that feminists don't need boyfriends

D She smiles sweetly and tells you she's already dating him

6 You've had a huge bust-up. Does your friend...

A Write you a five-page letter detailing what went wrong and how to make up

B Shout you down at first but then tell you sistas need to stick together

C She pretends nothing has happened and lets it blow over

D Gives you the ice queen treatment but apologises later

7

You have a girly bonding session. Does it involve...

A Judy Garland films back to back with the subtitles on so you can sing along

B A massive takeaway and gossip fest

C A night in discussing what it means to be a feminist at McKinley High

D A secret ante-natal class for your friend. She begs you not to tell

8

What's your friend's biggest secret?

A She's got two gay dads but wants to know who her mom is

B She acts all independent but would secretly like to fall in love

C Her stutter stops at home and she wishes she'd never started it

D Her pregnancy conception isn't so immaculate after all

MOSTLY As
Your bestie is Rachel

She is the person the phrase 'high maintenance' was invented for but if you can put in the time and effort needed to be her friend it'll definitely be worth it. Rachel is loyal when you need it, enthusiastic and helpful if you like a boy and a sympathetic listener if it all goes horribly wrong – as long as you're not standing between her and the spotlight of course. Just remember she's the star, so as long as you're happy being the side-kick you could be besties forever.

MOSTLY Cs
Your bestie is Tina

She's the person who made it OK to be you, the real you, not the person everyone expected you to be. So whether you dye your hair black and wear thick eyeliner or sit in the corner with your nose in a book, your bestie knows being different is being cool – whatever anyone else says. But while she truly believes that, it's up to you to help her stand up for herself. She might look brave and confident on the outside but all she really wants is to fit in, and she does... with you. So as long as she has you by her side, everything will be just fine.

MOSTLY Bs
Your bestie is Mercedes

Life will never be quiet when Mercedes is around – but then, you probably knew that already. She'll defend you as fiercely as she would herself, and just as loudly. But be warned, there's only ever room for one diva in the house. That doesn't mean you have to play second fiddle to her though, she might be all mouth on the outside but you know she's got a soft centre, and that's where you come in. Every time she tells you 'Come on girlfriend' just remember she needs to hear it too and for every bit of confidence she gives you, she relies on you for just as much. But that's what real friends are for isn't it?

MOSTLY Ds
Your bestie is Quinn

She's always thought the most important thing in life was to be popular – but now she's not quite so sure. After seeing things from the other side she knows how fast you can fall from the top of the tree, and what it's like at the bottom. But that's not a bad thing. Finally she's got some perspective, and she can give you some too. You've been by her side for the highs and now the lows so stick with it and you'll find your friendship just gets better and better.

glee

EPISODE 15

HOME

If Mercedes and Kurt think they've somehow softened up the cheer squad coach then they're sadly mistaken. Not even giving her a Madonna makeover was enough to court favour. Now as fully fledged members of the squad the pain has begun. She's been approached for a profile in *Splits* magazine and no cheerleader is safe from a drastic overhaul. Number one on her mauling list is gym-pants-clad buxom babe Mercedes. If she doesn't lose ten pounds and don a skirt she's off the team.

Meanwhile Sue has used further Figgins blackmailing credits to bagsy the auditorium. She says her squad will need it for the entire week preparing for their showcase. Glee Club are banned. Practising in their music room New Directions are not taking kindly to their unceremonious eviction. Puck suggests arson. Will promises to find them a new home to practise.

Will is scouring Lima for a place to practise and wanders into the local roller rink. There compering is none other than April Rhodes who is now the mistress of a strip-mall magnate and the proud owner of the roller rink he bestowed on her. She invites Will to

SONGS

'Fire' originally sung by *Bruce Springsteen*

'A House Is Not A Home'
originally sung by *Dionne Warwick*

'Home Sweet Home'
originally sung by *Carrie Underwood*

'Home' originally sung by *Stephanie Mills*

'One Less Bell To Answer/A House Is Not A Home' originally sung by *Barbra Streisand*

'Beautiful' originally sung by
Christina Aguilera

perform a duet of 'Fire' and offers use of the rink for free for Glee Club. When Will mentions he's getting a divorce April is suitably sympathetic. 'So you're free to date?' she gasps. 'And by date, I mean sleep with people? Have sex with people? People like me?' Well that was subtle. Will smiles, makes his excuses and leaves.

It's not gone well at the cheer squad weigh-in. Despondent Mercedes was trying her best to diet but instead of losing weight she's actually gained two pounds. She's got to take action. Santana and Brittany have even shared their secret slimming formula: the Sue Sylvester Master Cleanse (complete with vomiting agent). But hunger is making Mercedes hallucinate and she's imagining her friends as giant talking desserts dying to be eaten. When she eventually faints, reformed food obsessive Quinn has a word or two of advice for her. Mercedes is beautiful the way she is and has got to stop letting Sue control her life like this.

Back home Finn is upset. His mom Carole is giving away his dead dad's furniture. Turns out she has a new boyfriend – and it's Kurt's father, Burt. A shocked Finn finds out from Kurt that they met at a parent-teacher conference. Kurt omits to mention that it was he who played cupid. Why would he when he practically pushed the parents together in order to spend more time with Finn. It's clear he's fantasising about cosy room-shares before the term is out. At Glee rehearsals he practically serenades Finn with 'A House Is Not A Home'. Finn is mortified, knowing other people are aware of Kurt's unrequited love for him.

When Will visited the roller rink April expressed an interest in renting his apartment. But when she stops by 'to view it' Will notices she's brought an overnight bag. She says she's lonely and Will agrees she can sleep on the couch – but that doesn't stop her sneaking into Will's bed for a bit of handholding! Later, at rehearsals at the roller rink, Will tells April she should find a place of her own as she'll feel happier for it. For once April takes this advice graciously and says she'll break up with her sugar daddy.

It's a terse Finn who joins Kurt and their parents for a special dinner. His school pal looks like the cat that got the cream. Kurt's dad does his best to put Finn at ease. As he chats with Finn about football Kurt's satisfied smile is replaced by a scowl of jealousy. This was not the plan. Now he and Finn are united in their quest to break up their parents. But when Finn makes a scene at home, his mom tells him he's selfish. His father died sixteen years ago and this is the first time she's had a chance of happiness since.

The reporter from *Splits* magazine is not all he seems. Not only is he a *man* called Tracy, he's also a hard-hitting freelance investigative reporter looking for a scoop. As the lights dim and the cheerleaders take their positions, Mercedes walks out in her tracksuit pants and performs an unexpected monologue. 'How many of you feel like maybe you're not worth very much?' she asks addressing the crowd of teenagers. 'Or you're ugly, or you have too many pimples and not enough friends? Well, I felt all those things about myself at one time or another. Hell, I felt most of those things about myself today. And that just ain't right.' Her speech receives a standing ovation and then Mercedes launches into a rousing performance of 'Beautiful'. Sue naturally takes the credit when the reporter reveals he was blown away by the altruistic message from her cheerleading team.

Finn receives a visit from Burt who promises he is not trying to replace Finn's dad, he just wants to look after Finn's mom. As they settle down to watch a basketball game together they are watched on by a tearful Kurt who once again is stricken with insecurity about his own strained relationship with his dad.

April's lover passed away while she was attempting to dump him, and his wife has given her $2 million to keep schtum. She reveals to Will that she's donated some of the money to McKinley High. Glee Club will now be performing in the April Rhodes Civic Pavilion and New Directions will always have priority to use the auditorium. Hurrah!

EMMA PILLSBURY

Age: 30

Timid Emma is the quirky and jittery school counsellor with the cutest collection of twin-sets and a bad crush on fellow teacher Will.

As a little girl Emma had her heart set on being a dairy farmer but when she finally visited a dairy farm aged eight her brother pushed her into the runoff lagoon beginning a life-long obsession with hygiene. Emma now has to be clean at all times and won't go anywhere without her gloves, sanitising products and oral hygiene kit.

Emma is kind and caring but her struggle to be heard and hang-ups about physical relations often leave her frustrated. She worries that her lack of sexual experience makes her an inadequate counsellor but she has common sense by the bucket-load and often dishes out sage advice.

However Emma is in danger of settling for second best when she agrees to marry smitten football coach Ken Tanaka, despite not loving him. Ken later breaks up with her on their wedding day forcing Emma to face up to the truth – she is head over heels in love with Will.

Underneath her nervous exterior Emma has guts and a strong conviction for what is right and wrong. When she finally finds her voice she is motivated to speak out by an unlikely source – the person who ridicules her the most, Sue Sylvester.

After berating Will for cheating on her with Shelby, Emma starts to be more assertive generally, standing up for what she believes in and even squaring up to the school principal when he axes Glee Club.

Although she claims to be moving on, and has started to date her dentist, Will knows her passionate outburst to Figgins is a reflection of her feelings for him. He's right too! And when he kisses Emma all thoughts of hygiene suddenly disappear as the smitten counsellor falls into his arms.

Aww.

Love interests: Will, Ken Tanaka

Rivals: Terri, Sue Sylvester

Musical heroes: Julie Andrews

FACT! Emma hand polishes every grape before she eats it

glee EPISODE 16
BAD REPUTATION

What's this? Sue Sylvester is a school laughing stock?

When Sue sent Kurt to her office to fetch her hormone replacement injection she didn't count on him stumbling across an incriminating video. Now Sue's highly embarrassing attempts to recreate Olivia Newton-John's 'Physical' routine have been posted on the internet. It has already received over 170,000 comments. 'The man in this video looks like the champion cheerleading coach Sue Sylvester,' reads one.

Not only is Sue hurt, her ferocious reputation is in jeopardy. Suddenly all the staff and students who used to cower if she even looked at them are laughing in her face.

As Sue vents her spleen in Figgins' office she also brings a 'Glist' that is being posted around school to the principal's attention. The 'Who's Hot Who's Not' ranking lists the Glee clubbers in order of their sexual promiscuity. It ranks Quinn, Santana and Puck at the top while Rachel languishes at the bottom with minus five. The list was printed out using the password 'gleeclub'

and Figgins orders Will to find the student responsible. If no one owns up the entire Glee Club will be carpeted. But at rehearsals no one comes clean.

Will reveals their assignment this week is to rehabilitate songs that have been struck down with a bad reputation. He kicks this off with a performance of 'Ice Ice Baby' while the students join in with their best Vanilla Ice dance moves. Hurt by her minus-five ranking Rachel enlists Artie to help her make a video that will put paid to her squeaky-clean reputation. It's time for her to be 'musically promiscuous'.

Kurt, Artie, Mercedes and Tina also feel their 'free-falling reps' needs an overhaul and hatch a plan to create a scandal.

Sue is still struggling with her international ridicule and pays a visit to her sister Jean. She feels bad that she didn't do more to protect her when they were kids. Jean reminds her that there is always someone worse off you can help. Sue decides on her charity case *de jour* – it's Emma and it's high time she grew a backbone. To help Emma find her inner rage Sue

SONGS

'Ice Ice Baby'
originally sung by *Vanilla Ice*

'U Can't Touch This'
originally sung by *MC Hammer*

'Physical'
originally sung by *Olivia Newton-John*

'Run Joey Run'
originally sung by *David Geddes*

'Total Eclipse Of The Heart'
originally sung by *Bonnie Tyler*

reveals she bugged Will's apartment with baby monitors and has damning evidence of his make-out session with Shelby and sleepover with April. She advises her protégée to let Will 'have it' in a public setting. All fired up, Emma storms into the packed staff room to confront Will. He's busy consoling an elderly lady whose husband has just died but Emma loses it at him accusing him of 'getting them fresh off the rebound'. She labels him a slut and marches out again.

Keen to trash their reps, Kurt, Artie, Mercedes and Tina head for the library hell bent on anarchy. Brittany accompanies them as she's keen to improve her Glist ranking from number four. Dressed in MC Hammer harem pants the rebels then proceed to cause a stir in the library with an attitude-y Artie blasting out 'U Can't Touch This' with the four Glee clubbers pulling off some scorching moves around him. The librarian looks suitably outraged until the end when she declares their performance is 'cute'. She says she's going to talk to her pastor to see if they can perform at the Sunday service. Shucks. With their hopes of securing a 'bad-ass' reputation dwindling by the second Kurt decides on a last ditch attempt at coolness, they'll come clean about posting Sue's video online.

Meanwhile Sue is irritated to get a crank call from someone pretending to be Olivia Newton-John. She hangs up but the mystery caller rings back. It really is Olivia and she wants to meet Sue. So when Kurt fesses up and prepares to be blasted, the cheery coach just thanks him instead. Bemused, the Glee clubbers log

on to You Tube where they find out why Sue is feeling so jubilant. Olivia Newton-John has posted an updated version of her 'Physical' video, dueting with none other than one smug-looking Sue Sylvester. As the pair sing in blue sportswear, lycra-clad hunks work out all around them. And as a top-700 recording artist, Sue makes a tidy sum. During a visit to Jean she promises to donate the money to her sister's care home.

Will is still no nearer to discovering who posted the Glist but agrees that Rachel can screen her video. We know Rachel persuaded Puck to star in a video remake of 'Run Joey Run' and that during filming he'd tried it on, but Rachel rebuffed him. But that's not the half of it. As the cheesy video footage is aired Puck, Jessie and Finn all look on in disbelief. It seems La Berry has sneakily triple cast them to make it appear as if they are fighting over her. With dented egos the boys express their disgust and walk out. Nice one, Rach.

A flower-laden Will apologises to Emma and asks her to forgive him but she says she doesn't think they can go back to the way things were. Despondent, he goes back to his teacher duties and finally works out who created the list. It is clear that Quinn, whose school kudos is trickling away as she blooms, wanted to be noticed for something – even if the connotations are negative. Will confronts Quinn but doesn't have the heart to tell Figgins, but now the lists have stopped he manages to convince the principal to let the matter lie.

Unfortunately for Rachel, Jessie is determined to hold a grudge and promptly breaks up with her. The broken couple's angst is then conveyed as New Directions croon the hit 'Total Eclipse of the Heart'.

SUE SYLVESTER

Age: repeatedly claims to be 30

As the coach of McKinley High's award-winning cheerleading troupe, Sue will stop at nothing to scoop her 6th consecutive national title.

Whether it be blackmail, bribery, skulduggery or outright abuse Sue knows how she C's it and doesn't care who she tramples on to get where she wants to be.

When Glee Club inadvertently gets in the way of her budget, beloved cheer team or practice opportunities she reacts with fire and venom making Will public enemy number one.

There is nothing Sue enjoys more than ritually tormenting Will. She is razor sharp with her loaded put-downs and cuts a frightening figure as she storms the McKinley High halls in her array of colourful tracksuits.

Sue would like nothing more than for people to think that she is bad through and through but underneath it all she does have a heart (Just don't tell her you've noticed as she might be sick in your mouth).

She may come across as shockingly un-PC but she actually cares passionately about the welfare of those with disabilities. Her elder sister Jean has Down's syndrome and Sue privately dotes on her.

Despite giving the impression of being ruthlessly independent, Sue would actually like to find love. She is left burnt by news anchor Rod Remington after she mistakenly believes they are going steady and also feels humiliated that she allowed herself to daydream about Will being her trophy husband.

She may be hell bent on world domination – revelling in her cult status for her nightly TV segment Sue's Corner – but Sue also has morals. When she feels that New Directions are not being given a fair chance at Regionals she's prepared to speak up to the other judges – not that she'd ever tell Will that.

Likewise when Figgins cuts the club it is Sue who makes him give them another chance – even though Will's appreciation of her doing so makes her feel quite bilious.

Love Interests: Will Schuester, Principal Figgins, Rod Remington

Rivals: Will Schuester, Emma Pillsbury, Glee Club

Musical Heroes: Madonna, Olivia Newton-John

FACT! Sue owns a condo in Boca

glee EPISODE 17
LARYNGITIS

Uh-oh, mohawked Puck is making like Samson. He's shaved off his hair after his mom noticed a suspicious mole and now he's lost his power. Not only is nobody scared of him but a gaggle of much-maligned geeks even picked him up and tossed him in the dumpster. The worm has turned and Puck is fish food. If only there was a way he could get his mojo back? Peering out of the dumpster Puck sees Mercedes, now the school sweetheart after her cheerleading performance. In a flash of inspiration Puck decides she's his meal ticket to popular. 'Get ready, black girl whose name I can't remember,' he muses. 'The Puckster is about to make you his.' Lucky old Mercedes!

Elsewhere Rachel is feeling the pressure of life as a leading lady. She is popping vitamins left right and centre to keep her voice in tip-top condition but the strain is getting to her. With a hunch that some of the other Glee clubbers aren't singing during practices she does what all ruthless aspiring starlets would do – she bugs the choir room and gives Will a list of the non-singers. Apparently it's half the club. Less than impressed with his slacking choir Will demands an explanation. Finn admits he lost interest when all the male leads started going to Jessie, Santana is too busy looking hot, Quinn blames baby lethargy and Brittany is just struggling with the lyrics. Will decides that every Glee clubber must come up with a solo song that represents their voice to perform at the next rehearsal.

At Glee Club Rachel is the first to perform her song. She's chosen 'The Climb' to represent the obstacles she's overcome, by which she means her lacklustre teammates. As she begins to warble everyone is astounded. Her pitching is way off. Rachel has lost her voice!

After spotting his dad arriving at school to meet Finn to go to a football game, Kurt's jealous, and this is making him question his identity. He's swapped his usual flamboyant metrosexual wardrobe for baggie jeans, a flannel shirt, a vest and cap and for the assignment he chooses the song 'Pink Houses' – admittedly because it's about 'bold interior design' so not a complete change then.

Finn accompanies Rachel to see a doctor about her voice. The everdramatic Rachel fears she will never sing again. Her doctor says it's an inner-ear infection and tonsillitis. When he suggests taking the suckers out Rachel almost has heart failure. What if the operation causes irreparable damage? After a discussion about whether she should have the op or not Finn questions whether Rachel believes Jessie would stick around if she did end up a 'vocal cripple'. Rachel is adamant that she and Jessie still have a chance, prompting Finn to choose a moving solo of 'Jessie's Girl' for his assignment.

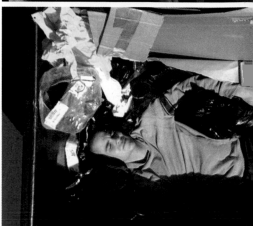

So far the Puckster's homing in on Mercedes has had no effect and she's remained gloriously disinterested, even when he told her she had 'curves like a Nissan ad'. Mercedes thinks they have nothing in common. So Puck is the next boy to attempt to woo the object of his (admittedly fickle)

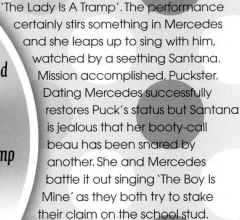

SONGS

'The Climb'
originally sung by *Miley Cyrus*

'Jessie's Girl' originally sung by *Rick Springfield*

'The Lady Is A Tramp'
originally sung by *Sammy Davis Jr*

'Pink Houses' originally sung by *John Mellencamp*

'The Boy Is Mine'
originally sung by *Brandy & Monica*

'One' originally sung by *U2*

'Rose's Turn' originally sung by
Ethel Merman

affections as he launches into a rendition of 'The Lady Is A Tramp'. The performance certainly stirs something in Mercedes and she leaps up to sing with him, watched by a seething Santana. Mission accomplished, Puckster. Dating Mercedes successfully restores Puck's status but Santana is jealous that her booty-call beau has been snared by another. She and Mercedes battle it out singing 'The Boy Is Mine' as they both try to stake their claim on the school stud.

Later Kurt sings 'Pink Houses', still decked out in his masculine attire. It is not a great performance and Will tells Kurt not to try and change who he is. However Brittany is intrigued by Kurt's new persona and offers to let him 'tap this'. Kurt takes Brittany home and makes out with her, rather uncomfortably, on the sofa. Pausing for air Kurt asks her what boys' lips taste like. 'Usually dip, sometimes burgers, or my armpits,' Brittany tells him matter-of-factly. They are interrupted by Kurt's dad who is confused to have come home to a sign on the doorknob reading: 'Do not enter under any circumstances, I'm making out with a girl.' He thought it was just one of Kurt's murder mystery dinners. Burt is understandably confused by Kurt's behaviour but tells him he is free to be whoever he is.

Finn catches sight of a dishevelled Rachel wandering aimlessly through the school corridors sporting pyjamas and messy hair. After three days her tonsils aren't any better so now she's going to have to have surgery which will totally ruin her whole life.

Fed up with her maudlin attitude, Finn takes her to meet his friend Sean, who was left paralysed after a football game went drastically wrong. Sean explains that losing something you love doesn't mean that life is over. There are always other things to live for: in his own case he's discovered that he loves to sing. A humbled Rachel returns to visit Sean, this time without Finn. She has her voice back and she wants to give him singing lessons once a week. Sean suggests they get started straight away and together they duet on 'One'.

Mercedes has made a radical decision. After witnessing Puck dumping geeks in the trash she has decided to abandon her new social status. Being an uber-popular cheerleader with a boyfriend who picks on nerds is not really her. She dumps Puck and quits the team.

Kurt is walking hand-in-hand with Brittany when his dad calls out to him. He's picking up Finn again for another sporting afternoon out. Burt explains that Carole thinks Finn benefits from spending time with him, but Kurt is once again hurt at being left out. Walking away Kurt begins a powerful rendition of 'Rose's Turn' culminating in the empty auditorium with a lone spectator clapping. Unbeknown to Kurt his father has been watching the whole time. Burt reveals he's cancelled his afternoon out with Finn to spend time with Kurt and doesn't want him to try and be something he's not any more. 'Your job is to be yourself,' he tells him, 'and my job is to love you, no matter what.'

I like to give impromptu concerts for the homeless. It's so important to give back.

JESSIE ST JAMES

Age: 18

As the lead singer of rival, champion show choir Vocal Adrenaline Jessie is a bit of a local celebrity thanks to his star quality and boyish good looks.

Jessie arrives on the scene when he meets Rachel 'accidentally' in a local library and woos her with a romantic duet of 'Hello'.

Rachel who is fresh from her Finn heartache is instantly smitten and agrees to go on a date.

Jessie proves to be a conundrum. While the Glee clubbers are suspicious of his intentions, Rachel is adamant that he is the real deal and at times he can be adorable, reeling off feel-good mantras to boost his girlfriend's confidence.

As he tells Rachel: 'You singing "Don't Cry For Me Argentina" in front of a sold-out crowd isn't a fantasy. It's an inevitability.'

But he also has a slippery side. When Rachel is unsure about sleeping with him he gets moody with her and it transpires he's on a secret mission to help Rachel identify Shelby as her mom. He admits he started off seeing his seduction of Rachel as an 'acting exercise' but has grown to have feelings for her. He tells Shelby he doesn't want to hurt her.

Yet his thirst for fame is clearly stronger than his loyalty to Rachel. Abandoning the New Directions right before Regionals to return to Vocal Adrenaline Jessie breaks Rachel's heart and then cruelly humiliates her. Whether he can redeem himself remains to be seen.

Love interests: Rachel

Rivals: Finn, New Directions

Musical heroes: Queen, Lionel Richie

FACT! He is unable to pull off a funk number

TERRI SCHUESTER

Age: 30 something

Former cheerleader Terri begins the first series married to her high school sweetheart Will and working part time at the local homeware store Sheets N' Things.

Despite having a doting and kind husband Terri has felt dissatisfied with her life for a while now. She was once the belle of McKinley High and misses her school popularity status. She also longs for a bigger home and a baby.

With Will busy at work and her marriage hitting a bit of a rocky patch Terri fears she'll lose her husband so is delighted when she develops symptoms of pregnancy. She and Will have wanted children for a while and a classic Band-Aid baby could help reinvigorate their marriage.

But when it turns out to be a phantom pregnancy she doesn't have the heart to crush Will's dreams. Instead, largely influenced by her devious sister Kendra, she creates a web of lies – faking her bump, sonogram and secretly planning to adopt Quinn's baby.

Although Terri is selfish and manipulative her actions are largely fuelled by insecurity. She loves Will and worries that she'll lose him to Emma. Sadly if she'd just been able to tell the truth she might have kept hold of him.

Now divorced Terri is trying to be a better person by helping Finn, one of her employees, with his Glee assignments. Yet we can't help thinking she fancies a little cougar time too – Grrr.

> *I mean, I'm weak, and I'm selfish, and I let my anxiety rule my life, but you know I wasn't always that way...*

Love interests: Will, Finn

Rivals: Emma, April

FACT! Terri is allergic to nuts

THE KURT HUMMEL STYLE GUIDE

(makeovers are like crack to me)

Ballads

Mattress

Every moment of your life is an opportunity for fashion.

I've known who I was since I was five. I adapted. Being different made me stronger. And at the end of the day, it's what's going to get me out of this cow town.

There's never an excuse for stirrup pants!

You know why they call them slushies...? Because your butt looks like one if you have too many of them.

Mercedes is black; I'm gay. We make culture.

I admit I like a challenge as much as the next guy, but Rachel somehow manages to dress like a grandmother and a toddler at the same time.

Night time skin care is a big part of my post-game ritual.

The key is to never wax above the eyebrow. Always shape from below.

It's a unitard. Guys wear them to, uh, work out nowadays. Do sports. They wick sweat from the body... They're jock-chic.

My secret? Duck fat.

Vitamin D

Sectionals

Mattress

Hairography

glee EPISODE 18

DREAM ON

Once upon a time, in the days before he even met Sue Sylvester, Will Schuester had a high-school rival called Bryan Ryan. Bryan was the Jessie St James of Glee Club. He was two years older, cooler and got all the hottest girls. Worst of all he mercilessly picked on Will. Now Bryan Ryan is sat in Figgins's office and once again he's hell bent on making Will miserable.

As the newest member of the school board he is doing a curriculum audit and plans to axe some of the arts programmes – starting with Glee Club. Will is outraged. 'But you were in the Glee Club!' he protests. Ryan reveals how his Glee Club-induced desire for fame and fortune led him to disappointment, despair and a crack addiction. Then he found God, set up a 'used Hummer' dealership and formed a 'show choir conversion group'. Ryan says he wants to meet New Directions and make sure Will isn't encouraging them to pursue impossible aspirations. This he does by encouraging each pupil to write down their dream.

Rachel wants to be a 'huge star', Puck is dreaming of a '3some' and Quinn scribbles 'no stretch marks'. When they are done Ryan snatches up Artie's piece of paper and tosses it into the bin. 'Your dreams are never going to happen,' Ryan barks. 'Ninety-one percent of you will spend your entire lives living in Allen County, Ohio.' As the kids look crestfallen Ryan adds that showbiz dreams are the most unrealistic of them all, hailing Will as the prime example of a star wannabe who never made it. His brutal pep talk leaves Tina sobbing.

Later in the library Tina tells Artie that she retrieved his crumpled dream from the bin. Reading that he wants to be a 'dancer' she wants to work with him on a special routine at this week's Glee Club. When they rehearse Artie is determined to try tap dancing but his attempts to stand with braces goes drastically wrong as he topples over and lands, helpless, on the floor. Embarrassed and humiliated he yells at Tina to leave him alone.

SONGS

'Daydream Believer'
originally sung by *The Monkees*

'Piano Man' originally sung by *Billy Joel*

'Dream On' originally sung by *Aerosmith*

'Safety Dance'
originally sung by *Men Without Hats*

'I Dreamed A Dream'
originally sung by *Patti LuPone*

'Dream A Little Dream Of Me'
originally sung by *Mama Cass*

Determined to save Glee, Will decides to try and win Bryan over and invites him for a beer. As they chat about Bryan's former stud status, he admits the one girl he always held a torch for but could never have was Will's ex-wife. Then, softened up by alcohol, he makes a revelation. He still longs to perform and makes clandestine trips to Broadway behind his wife's back. Together with Will he performs 'Piano Man' – the song he soloed at Sectionals in 1992 – in the bar. Will says they should both audition for a local production of *Les Miserables*.

Rachel has confessed to Jessie that her true dream is to meet her birth mother. After researching the 1994 work schedules of Broadway stars she is convinced that Patti LuPone is her mom. Jessie is not so sure. Later, when Rachel is sifting through boxes of paperwork from the attic looking for clues about her birth mother, Jessie slips a cassette tape labelled 'From Mother to Daughter' into one of the boxes when she's not looking. He urges shocked Rachel to play it.

Tina has apologised to Artie for pushing him to dance and has been researching spinal cord surgery. She's printed off some research for him to read. It's got Artie's hopes up and at the mall Artie picks up some tap shoes. Suddenly he gets out of his chair and sings and dances his way through an impressive flash-mob style routine of 'Safety Dance'. But alas it was all a dream. Poor Artie.

The truce between Will and Bryan disintegrates once more as they both audition for the lead role in *Les Mis* of Jean Valjean. They embark on a sing-off, both crooning 'Dream On' for the director. Also, Bryan has found someone new to argue about budgets with – Sue Sylvester. As the conversation gets increasingly heated Bryan announces that Sue is turning him on. They head off for some 'anger sex'. Still high off his audition (and maybe his time with Sue) Bryan tells the Glee kids their club is safe and he has even allocated them some of the cheer team's budget. But his generosity is short lived as Sue comes in to congratulate Will on snagging the lead role in *Les Mis* and Bryan for scooping the 'one-line' part of 'townsperson'. Sue, once again, has been meddling. A dejected Bryan immediately retracts his generous offer, announcing he is cutting the programme. That is, until Will panders to him, handing over his Jean Valjean role.

Jessie is seen sneaking into the car of his former Vocal Adrenaline coach. We learn he is on a secret mission to help Rachel discover that Shelby is her biological mother, as legally Shelby can't contact her directly until after her eighteenth birthday. Jessie admits that, although he started out using his Rachel 'seduction' as an acting exercise, he now has feelings for her. When he next sees Rachel, a determined Jessie makes Rachel listen to the tape, which transpires to be a recording of her 'mom' singing 'I Dreamed A Dream'. An emotional Rachel joins in and then breaks down.

Artie books in for a session with Emma to talk about his hope of walking one day. Emma tells him that it is unlikely to happen anytime soon and Artie can't hide his disappointment. He decides it's time to face up to his limitations. He urges Tina to dance with another member of New Directions but to sing the song for him. A reluctant Tina tap dances with Mike Chang as Artie sings 'Dream A Little Dream of Me'. Mike may have the moves but Artie has her heart.

'...You need twelve kids to qualify for Regionals. Last time I looked, you only had five and a half.' Sue

THEATRICALITY

Figgins has summoned Tina to his office. He is concerned that vampire fever is descending on the school and for some reason thinks the children are in danger of transforming into vampires. He believes Tina with her penchant for goth wear is a likely candidate for turning. He wants her to dress more conservatively immediately.

Will tries to reason with the principal to no avail so Tina has to turn up to Glee Club in her boring non-goth attire. She feels deflated so the others make suggestions of new looks including biker chick, cowgirl and Catholic schoolgirl. Brittany thinks she should dress up as a kid's burger without the onions.

Yikes, Burt, Carole and Kurt have organised a surprise 'We're all moving in together!' party for Finn. This news naturally goes down like a lead balloon with Finn. And it only gets worse... Burt is going to build Finn a new room but until then he gets to share with Kurt, who's not at all in love with him, oh no.

Regionals are just weeks away when Rachel reveals she has discovered that Vocal Adrenaline have been stocking up on Christmas lights and red Chantilly lace. Kurt, Mercedes and Tina gasp in horror. This can only mean one thing. Vocal Adrenaline are going 'Gaga' for Regionals. It's agreed that this week they will work on Lady Gaga numbers.

Later a Vocal Adrenaline-obsessed Rachel sneaks into the Carmel High auditorium with Mercedes and Quinn where Shelby is putting them through their paces. She chastises her charges for not possessing true 'theatricality' and performs 'Funny Girl' to emphasise her point. Rachel is left gobsmacked. Recognising her mother's voice immediately she wanders down to introduce herself as Shelby's long-lost daughter. Mission accomplished. During a heart-to-heart Rachel tells Shelby she feels thirsty. This is largely because when she was sad as a little girl her dads would always hand her a glass of water. She says it got to the point where she didn't know whether she was sad or just thirsty. Shelby is clearly uncomfortable with this intimacy and dashes off promising to call Rachel.

At Glee rehearsals Mercedes and Quinn gossip about Rachel's news, and wonder whether she is now going to defect to Vocal Adrenaline. When Miss Berry arrives, New Directions' superstar reassures them she'll be staying put, but judging by her Gaga garb it's clear her mind is elsewhere. While all the other girls and Kurt are decked out in fabulous Lady Gaga fashions (which have already made Tina and Kurt the target of the school bullies), Rachel has hordes of stuffed animals stapled to her dress. Overlooking her menagerie fashion frock horror they launch into a performance of 'Bad Romance'.

SONGS

'Funny Girl'
originally sung by *Barbra Streisand*

'Bad Romance'
originally sung by *Lady Gaga*

'Shout It Out Loud'
originally sung by *Kiss*

'Beth' originally sung by *Kiss*

'Poker Face'
originally sung by
Lady Gaga

Poor Finn, he's not having an easy time. After complaining to Will about yet another overtly feminine Glee assignment he is ridiculed by the same thugs who had a pop at Kurt and Tina earlier. They accuse him of catching 'the gay' from Kurt and tell him Glee is making him bisexual. At the next Glee rehearsal the boys, minus Kurt, surprise everyone when they arrive decked out in black with heavily made-up faces and huge platform boots. Will has allowed them to channel a rock band and they take to the stage to perform 'Shout It Out Loud'.

As well as helping out Finn, St Schue, as he is fast shaping up to be, has summoned Shelby to a meeting as he is worried Rachel is going to be left disappointed by her reunion. A jubilant Rachel had turned up to rehearsals in a new Gaga ensemble made for her by her 'mom'. Shelby admits she's now unsure about taking on a teenage daughter and Will asks her to be straight with Rachel.

Over at Chez Hummel, where Finn is now sharing a room with Kurt, the two teenagers got into an awkward conversation about the jocks who had once again targeted Kurt about his Gaga-wear. When he asked Finn to stick up for him, a stressed Finn suggested that Kurt should try blending in more. As Finn attempted to remove his KISS make-up Kurt leaned in to help, causing Finn to freak out and storm off. So Kurt has decided to make amends the only way he knows how. Uh-oh. He's only gone and transformed the room he shares with Finn into a theatrical Moroccan boudoir and a paranoid Finn believes he's hell bent on seduction.

Blowing a gasket Finn labels Kurt's choice of interiors and furnishings 'faggy'. A horrified Burt overhears Finn's 'poisonous' tirade and tells him to leave immediately.

It's an emotional Glee Club the next day, with Puck, who previously had the wonderful idea of naming his unborn daughter Jack Daniels, singing a song for Quinn – 'Beth'. He thinks it would be a nice name for their daughter and a moved Quinn agrees that Puck can be at the baby's birth.

Afterwards as Rachel is alone in the auditorium she is visited by Shelby. She knows her 'mom' has come to say goodbye. They agree that without shared stories of Rachel's childhood it is difficult to bond. They part on amicable terms with Shelby giving Rachel a water glass with a gold star on it and them singing a mournful acoustic version of 'Poker Face' together.

Fed up by being told what to wear Tina takes drastic action. Dressing up as a vampire she pounces on Figgins in the school corridor. Warning him that her father is the 'king of the vampires', she instructs him that he will let her wear her lady demon clothes or her dad will fly into his bedroom and bite his face off. A terrified Figgins agrees to her terms.

At Glee a clearly mortified Finn had tried to talk to Kurt but to no avail so he makes amends later in the day. Kurt is about to come a cropper courtesy of the football team when Finn jumps to his rescue emblazoned in a red rubber Lady Gaga dress. The other Glee clubbers are right behind him causing the jocks to scarper.

'Lady Gaga is a woman. She's only the biggest pop act to come along in decades. She's boundary-pushing, the most theatrical performer of our generation. And she changes her look faster than Brit changes sexual partners.' *Kurt*

Rivals: Sue, Tina

Love interests: Sue, also appears captivated by Shelby

FACT! Figgins once modelled for a Mumbai Air video demonstrating how to put on anti-clotting stockings.

For several years in my early twenties, I dressed up as Elvis.

PRINCIPAL FIGGINS

Age: unknown

As the principal of McKinley High, Figgins often finds himself in the middle of fierce battles between his warring staff Sue and Shue.

While trying to be fair, Figgins changes loyalties like the rest of us have hot dinners and has made some very odd decisions – like hiring Terri to be the school nurse when she had no formal qualifications and banning Tina from wearing her 'vampire' goth wear.

But Figgins is certainly not as strict as he makes out: he secretly enjoyed the X-rated Glee Club performance of 'Push It', but feels he has to tow the line to keep the parents happy.

When Sue blackmails him, drugging him and then takes incriminating pictures of him in her bed, he feels compelled to do what she wants – even blasting Madonna out of the school tannoy.

But with Sue having promised to bring her blackmail campaign to an end perhaps Figgins can now restore some authority in his own school.

KEN TANAKA

Age: early 40s?

Ken is the coach of the McKinley High Football Club and endures the daily disappointment of always being the underdog.

His football team are not a patch on Sue's champion cheer squad and the object of his affections, Emma, is madly in love with his better-looking colleague, Will.

Although at one point Ken is friends with Will, joining him in Acafellas and helping him to recruit new male singers from the football team, he soon turns on him out of jealousy.

Ken has persuaded a reluctant Emma to marry him with the promise of a life clean from loneliness and sadness but can't stand the way she continually goes gooey-eyed over Will. He hates being the consolation prize.

When Emma delays their wedding to take the Glee Club to Sectionals it is the final straw for Ken. He breaks up with her, gaining forty pounds and not bothering to shower. Poor Ken.

I don't know a lot about relationships. Most of mine are short and flame out once the sex goes.

Rivals: Will

Love interests: Emma

FACT! Ken has at least seventy-four flaws

MCKINLEY FOOTBALL

glee EPISODE 20
FUNK

Turns out that double-crossing Jessie has only gone and transferred back to Carmel High. And to add insult to injury, now here he is, bold as brass, performing a rather excellent rendition of 'Another One Bites The Dust' in the McKinley auditorium. And Vocal Adrenaline's parting gift is to cover the choir room in toilet paper too. Artie says it's a Carmel tradition to psych out the rivals and spin them into a funk before the competition.

As they clean up Sue reveals it was none other than she who let Vocal Adrenaline in. She's sizing up the choir room for a trophy annex. She wants it to look like Elvis's gold record room at Graceland but with 'fewer morbidly obese white women waddling around and crying'. Sue says New Directions are 40-1 underdogs at Regionals. An angry Will asks to see Sue's trophy and then smashes it. Not that Sue is bothered: 'Trophies are like herpes. You try to get rid of them but they keep on coming.'

Will and Terri finalise their divorce sadly but amicably. It prompts Will to talk to the kids about regrets. He wants the kids to have no regrets no matter what happens at Regionals but thinks they need to fight fire with fire. Finn and Puck make a silent pact to defend the honour of New Directions and are next seen slashing Vocal Adrenaline's tyres. When news of their 'felony' reaches Figgins he wants to expel them but Shelby relents. She won't press charges if they pay for the damage. When Will says this will bankrupt Glee Club Finn promises he and Puck will get jobs and pay the money back within a month. They take a job in Sheets N' Things where their boss appears to be having a cougar moment with Finn who clearly reminds her of a young Will.

When a depressed Will tells former show choir coach Sandy that Glee is hanging by a thread Sandy tells him that Vocal Adrenaline have a weakness. The next day Will reveals their new secret weapon to a down-hearted Glee club. 'Vocal Adrenaline has never once done a funk number,' he grins.

Will's got another score to settle too. That evening in a contrived moment he stares in wonder at Sue

SONGS

'Another One Bites The Dust'
originally sung by *Queen*

'Tell Me Something Good'
originally sung by *Rufus*

'Loser' originally sung by *Beck*

'It's A Man's, Man's, Man's World'
originally sung by *James Brown*

'Good Vibrations' originally sung by
Marky Mark and the Funky Bunch

'Give Up The Funk'
originally sung by *Parliament*

and compliments her on looking radiant. Sue agrees she looks good and appears to like the compliment. Will asks her to listen to a funk number he's been working on and let him know if it's too racy. Cue a saucy Schue crooning and wiggling his hot buns in the clearly flustered coach's direction to 'Tell Me Something Good'. Ooh err missus!

Meanwhile Sue is having impure thoughts of her own – about Will. Will doesn't help by bringing her flowers to match her tracksuit and her favourite appletini carbo gels. He says he'd like to take her to dinner. Adorned in a burgundy tracksuit accessorised with a pearl necklace Sue waits for Will. Eventually the waitress tells her she's been stood up. When an angry Sue bangs on Will's door and he explains he's tried to play nice but cruelty was the only way to get her attention.

Days later and Sue apparently won't get out of bed. Santana is sobbing in the corridor and the other cheerleaders are wandering around aimlessly. Will pays a visit to Sue's trophy-clad home. Her maid reveals that Sue is in a bad way, she's even refusing her protein shakes. Sue's had enough: she's devoted her life to the kids and feels she has nothing to show for it. Will apologises and persuades her to return to school.

Having asked to go first, Quinn warms up for her funk number by talking about the strains of pregnancy and the prejudice teenage moms-to-be face. She is joined by the Unwed Mothership Connection to perform 'It's a Man's, Man's, Man's World'. Afterwards Mercedes offers her a place to stay if living with Puck is getting to her. Finn, Puck and Mercedes also perform their 'Funk' number 'Good Vibrations' by Marky Mark and The Funky Bunch. Will says it's not funk, it's rap. Artie thinks they're doing the wrong songs because they're clinically depressed.

After receiving a call from Jessie, Rachel dashes to the parking lot, clearly dreaming of a romantic reunion. Then some rotter pelts an egg at her. And then another. And another. It's Vocal Adrenaline. As Jessie takes in the sight of a miserable egg-splattered Rachel, he simmers 'I loved you,' before crushing a final egg on Rachel's forehead. Puck and Finn want to rearrange Jessie's face in revenge but Will stops them, saying that he knows from experience that making someone else suffer doesn't make your pain go away. Instead he calls Jessie on Rachel's phone and instructs Vocal Adrenaline to meet in their auditorium at 3 o'clock on Friday.

Sue has just won her sixth consecutive Nationals title. She speedily arrives at Will's front door complete with her new giant shiny trophy. She gloats that she plans to install it in the choir room as a daily reminder of his 'failings as a man and educator'. She gives Will a choice, he can avoid this fate if he kisses her on the lips with tongue. Will for some unfathomable reason seems to think this is a price worth paying but just as he puckers up Sue recoils. 'Even your breath stinks of mediocrity,' she simmers. 'And it's making me sick.'

It's 3 o'clock on Friday and Vocal Adrenaline are seated in the auditorium. Rachel saunters on to the stage to address them: 'We decided the only way to truly funkify you is to show you the one thing we know you can't do. So enjoy!' And with that New Directions blaze on to the stage to blast out an attitude-y, lyrical assault on their rivals. Jessie looks horrified as Puck cheerfully quips 'See you at Regionals!'

You're right, Will. I have been trying to destroy your club with a conviction I can only call 'religious'.

[Will] I spend large segments of each day picturing you choking on food. And I recently contacted an exotic animal dealer because I had a very satisfying dream that the two of us went to a zoo and I shoved your face into one of those pink inflamed monkey butts that weeps lymph.

[Will] I may buy a small diaper for your chin, because it looks like a baby's ass .

It's like Madonna once said: 'I'm tough, I'm ambitious, and I know what I want, and if that makes me a bitch, OK.' I'm pretty sure she stole that line from one Sue Sylvester.

THAT'S HOW SUE C'S IT

Sometimes people ask me, 'Sue, how come you're so sensitive to minorities?' Well, I'll tell you why. Because I know firsthand how hard it is to struggle as a minority in America today.

[Will] Your delusions of persecution are a telltale sign of early stage paranoid schizophrenia.

[Brittany and Santana] You may be two of the stupidest teens I've ever encountered – and that's saying something.

I for one think intimacy has no place in a marriage. Walked in on my parents once, and it was like seeing two walruses wrestling.

Caning works. And I think it's about time we did a little more of it right here. And to all those naysayers out there who say, 'That's illegal; you can't strike children on their bare buttocks with razor-sharp bamboo sticks,' well, to them, I say, 'Yes, we cane.'

[Santana and Brittany] This is what we call a total disaster, ladies. I'm going to ask you to smell your armpits. That's the smell of failure and it's stinking up my office. I'm revoking your tanning privileges for the rest of the semester.

[Emma] You take weird little strides when you walk as if you were raised in Imperial Japan and someone bound your feet.

Sue's names for Emma

Well, it's simple, Arlene. You don't deserve the power of Madonna. You have none of her self-confidence, her power over her body, or her sexual magnetism.

Ellen, that blouse is insane.

Ella, you're crippled by mental illness. Your compulsions have estranged you from your own feelings. You nearly married a gym teacher who's more gravy than man.

glee
EPISODE 21
JOURNEY

Did we really just hear Sue casually mentioning to Schue that she's going to be a judge at Regionals? Turns out that being the 'Michael Jordan of Cheerleading' has somewhat enhanced Sue's status – and some punk thought it fitting to invite her to be a 'celebrity' judge at Regionals. As Principal Figgins insists, there's nothing he can do – apart from remind Will that Glee Club will be disbanded if they don't get placed. Way to rub it in, pal. Naturally news of Sue's judging role goes down a treat at the first annual New Directions set list nominations party and just about everyone seems to be weeping.

Worried about his downcast charges Will asks Emma for guidance. She seems a little weary but tells him that surely the feeling of doing something you love is better than winning or losing. Then she casually mentions she's dating her dentist. There's only so much bad news a man can take and driving home Will is reduced to tears as the sounds of 'Don't Stop Believin'' filter through the radio.

Good job Finn is having a little more luck. Finding Rachel he bursts into a rousing speech about how together they are going to rally the troops to go forth and win this thing. Rachel immediately leans forward and kisses him. Atta girl!

At their final pep-talk before the big day, Will has dried his eyes and is making a steely attempt to motivate the kids. 'I was gonna quit once, but you guys brought me back with "Don't Stop Believin'". It was a nine, but we are going to make it a ten.' Gird your loins rock fans, the Gleesters are going to do a medley.

So finally the 2010 Midwest Regional Show Choir Championship is here. Celebrity judges Josh Groban, Olivia Newton-John, Rod Remington and Sue Sylvester prepare themselves for an afternoon of first-class entertainment from the region's most talented teenagers. Indiana's finest, Aural Intensity, are up first with a mash-up of the songs of Olivia Newton-John and Josh Groban. Dirty rotten suck-asses.

Outside the auditorium Rachel and Finn prepare for their performance. Rachel tells him to 'break a leg,' while Finn blurts out that he loves her! Smiling they both enter the hall from different sides of the stage skipping through the crowd singing 'Faithfully'. Running up on stage they are joined by the other New Directions harmonising into 'Anyway You Want It'. As New Directions segue into 'Don't Stop Believin'', Quinn's mom sneaks into the auditorium to watch her daughter's spine-tingling performance with teary pride. Backstage she greets Quinn remorsefully, tells her she's left her father as he was having an affair with a 'tattooed freak'. She wants Quinn to come home and suggests they can turn the guest room into a nursery. But Quinn is unable to answer as her waters just broke. Panic stations!

As Vocal Adrenaline take to the stage blasting out 'Bohemian Rhapsody' Quinn is rushed to hospital with Puck, her mom and several Glee clubbers in hot pursuit including Mercedes who she tells doctors she wants with her. Between the panting and groaning, Quinn screams at a very pale-looking Puck, 'You suck, you suck, you suck.' Finally Quinn gives birth to a bouncing baby daughter.

Meanwhile Rachel, who has stayed behind at the auditorium, finds Shelby in a dressing room. She asks her to transfer to McKinley High to co-coach New

Directions. But Shelby says she is leaving the heady highs of show-choiring behind. She wants to have a family. 'I missed out on my chance with you,' she reveals. 'I can't let that happen again.'

In the judging room Olivia is offended that only Aural Intensity chose to honour her 'in song'. Josh Groban seems more interested in finding out whether Sue is single but says New Directions had a lot of heart. The one voice of reason is Sue but the other three overrule her, what with her not being a proper celebrity and all that.

So the results are in and the teams take to the stage. Aural Intensity are runners up. The tension builds as the two remaining rival schools await their fate. And the winner is... VOCAL ADRENALINE! New Directions can't hide their disappointment. They didn't even place. Glee Club is over.

Back at the maternity wing Puck and Quinn are admiring their daughter. Shelby appears next to them gazing through the glass at the newborn babies... By the time New Directions are back at school, Shelby will be at the hospital signing the adoption papers for her new baby daughter – a little girl called Beth.

So, it's back to McKinley High, and Will is amazed to see Emma screaming at Figgins. 'He's already given the choir room to the Mock UN,' she vents. Will is amazed by Emma's passion for the club and takes a chance. 'I love you Emma and you love me,' he tells her. Then he kisses her.

Will is summoned to the auditorium by his Glee kids. One by one they reveal how being in New Directions has changed their lives. 'We don't care what the judges say, we won because we had you as a teacher,' Rachel tells Will who dissolves into tears as the kids perform 'To Sir With Love'.

But guess what? The show's not over until Sue Sylvester springs. This time she's caught Schue unawares with an uncharacteristic display of kindness. She's only gone and persuaded Figgins to let Glee Club have one more year. The news that Glee is saved is met with whoops of joy as Will sings a beautiful version of 'Over The Rainbow' for his beloved pupils. All's well that ends well. Check you next semester!

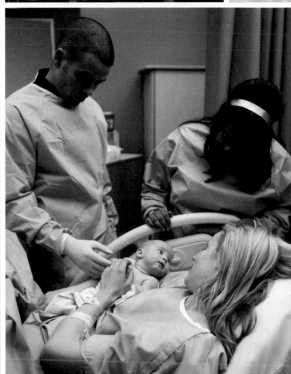

'One day, all of you are going to be gone. And all of this, all of us, will be nothing but a hazy memory. It will take you a second to remember everyone's name. Someone will have to remind you of the songs we sung, the solos you got or didn't get. Life only really has one beginning and one end, and the rest is just a whole lot of middle. And I love you guys too much to let you not make the most of it.' *Will*

CALLING ALL gleeks!

There are three official Glee novels that no self-respecting Gleek will want to be without.

GLEE: THE BEGINNING
£6.99
Available now
978 0 7553 7737 4

Get more of your favourite characters in this official Glee prequel! All great performances deserve a warm-up! Enroll early at McKinley High to find out what went on before New Directions was even a glimmer in Mr Schuester's eye. When did Rachel first decide Finn was more than just a jock? When did Puck and Quinn start their secret romance? And how did the fledgling Glee Club function without a fearless leader? Hint: It wasn't exactly a perfect melody. Break out the gold stars and refill the frozen drinks: it's time to find out what happened to all your favourite characters *before* the show-mance began.

GLEE: FOREIGN EXCHANGE
£6.99
Available in February
978 0 7553 7738 1

Can Rachel Berry rock a beret? McKinley High goes international when a French glee club comes to town in the second original Glee novel. Kurt gets an entourage, Finn falls for a new girl, and Puck learns that some moves are lost in translation in this hilarious culture-clash story.

GLEE: SUMMER BREAK
£6.99
Available in July
978 0 7553 7739 8

Mr Schuester doesn't want the Glee Club to lose its momentum over summer break, so he's talked Rachel, Finn and the crew into running a singing workshop for local kids.